To Amaae,
Mivvy
Love,
Mac and Manju

AN ELEPHANT KISSED

MY WINDOW

AND OTHER STORIES FROM THE TEA
PLANTATIONS OF SOUTH INDIA

B & W

M RAVINDRAN & SAAZ AGGARWAL

B & W

An elephant kissed my window
and other stories from the tea plantations of South India

Published by **black-and-white fountain**
2 Flemington Terrace, Clover Village, Wanowari, Pune 411040, India
First reprint November 2019
ISBN No. 978-93-83465-14-9
Cover image of Anaimudi Estate, Mudis, by Sangeetha Jairam
Editorial inputs Arjun Ravindran, Carolyn Hollis, KS Medappa, M Unni, Paran Balakrishnan,
Ravi Savur, Senthil Chengalvarayan and Vidya Kumaraswamy.
Book design and cover design Veda Aggarwal
Text and original images Saaz Aggarwal
Copyright © Saaz Aggarwal 2019
Silhouette graphics from Edward Lear's *Indian Journals*
on pages 43, 75, 126, 138, 145, 148, 169, 185, 199
For feedback and inquiries email blackandwhitefountain@gmail.com

CONTENTS

A NOTE ON THE STYLE USED IN THIS BOOK

This book follows a language style on the spectrum between British and American usage, a middle-ground generally considered acceptable in the globalization of the language. It chooses the idiomatic flow of contemporary English, lenient of an assortment that might include 'programme', 'organization', 'ton' and others, as relevant or convenient.

To give the reader the experience of a historically authentic setting, names of places later renamed (Ceylon, Madras, Bombay and others) have been retained as they were in the period presented. Captions of images display names of people from left to right. Abbreviations do not use full stops. Punctuation and spelling in the quotes excerpted from archival documents have been retained as in the original. While measurement uses the metric system, pounds and feet were the standard in the early period covered in this book, so miles and kilometres nestle side by side. More about measurement on page 120.

The non-English words in this book, being words that emerge from the community the book is documenting, have not been italicized, although meanings have been provided. It may be noted that the gazetteers present Indian words (such as janmabhogam and others) in straight face and meanings may be derived from context. Planting jargon, including words such as 'labour', 'lines', 'pluckers', 'cumblies', has been retained.

The font Bembo Std is used for Ravindran's stories, while text from other contributors appears in Avenir Book, to alert the reader to a change in voice. Archival documents are presented in Travelling Typewriter, to provide a sense of stepping into the past.

WALKING ON FIRE

It was bitterly cold that morning, and a thin layer of frost covered the earth. I got out of my new Standard Herald car at TR Bazaar, and walked with Thimma down to the temple, where he ran to join his parents, quickly spotting his mother in the crowd.

The fire had been blazing all night in front of the temple. I stood at a distance from the long bed of heated embers, neatly levelled to receive its guests, rubbing my hands together for warmth. Any closer and the heat would have been uncomfortable. A crowd of workers stood around it too, some squatting in groups looking away from the flare, while others sauntered around, shielding their eyes from it with their hands. Those tending the fire were clearly wilting in the heat. They had been stoking large quantities of firewood, burning it down all night to the cinders that had now been arranged into an ordered bed about 12m long, 1m wide and 30cm deep. Another group was pouring buckets of water on the red-hot ground around. Steam spewed as water met scorched earth and cooled it.

The temple priest rang a large bronze bell in his hand and made offerings of rice, bananas, and coconut. He walked around the bed, sprinkling holy water to sanctify it, stopping at intervals to pick up and drop handfuls of burning coals with his bare hands, as easily as if they were marbles. People in the watching crowd whispered to each other and nodded in awed approval: surely this superhuman feat was an indication that the gods were on his side!

The firewalkers were ready. They had spent the last forty days preparing themselves, fasting and praying in a state of purity. Each day, after completing their work on the estate, they had met at the temple and chanted prayers together under the direction of the priest. Frugal meals were brought from their homes to the temple, where they ate together. At night, they slept on its veranda, a strongly-bonded team whose closeness shielded them from temptation towards any immoral activity.

Having spent the previous night cloistered inside the temple, prevented from falling asleep by continuously chanting prayers, they were now immersed in the final ritual cleansing in the river below. As each one pulled himself out of the river, his forehead was anointed with bhasmam – ceremonial ash – and vermilion, and a garland of jasmine and marigold flowers was placed around his neck. Some smeared themselves all over with the ash. Together they climbed up the river bank to the temple to the increasing tempo of the high-pitched kettle drums traditionally used in temples in this area, some grimacing, others wearing vacant grins, seemingly in hypnotic trances, and trooped towards the bed of burning coals.

As they stepped onto it, loud cheers rose from the crowd. While some ran across, taking just a few long strides, others ambled, ankle-deep in burning coals. We watched, entranced, and I was horrified to see Thimma break away from his mother's hold and run to join them. She screamed in horror, raising her hands to her face as he stepped on to the bed of hot coals and ran determinedly across it, reaching the end just as successfully as the others.

To my eyes, Thimma had achieved a miracle, but for his parents and the other workers, and particularly for the priest, temple committee and the elders who guard the festival tradition, he had committed an atrocity. The child had leapt onto the consecrated fire without any of the essential ritual purifications. He would later explain that he had seen someone standing at the other end of the bed of fire, beckoning to him to join the firewalkers and, though he knew better, the summons had filled him with urgency he was unable to resist. Much did his mother plead that Thimma had been blessed with a vision; he was soundly thrashed anyway by the temple elders. Surely it was important to set an example to anyone else who might try to gate-crash the sacred ritual.

The firewalkers are boys and men who have committed themselves to the sanctifying Kondam ritual as penance to the gods. They come from families who have faced a hardship, perhaps a marriage which has not yet resulted in children, or a financial crisis, or disease or the untimely death of a family member. And they have been nominated by the head of the family to take part in the Kondam as an offering to Mariamman, the demanding deity. Occasionally a young person decides to take part of their own volition.

Most of the participants complete the ritual safely, but it is an inherently risky ritual and sometimes there are accidents. I was watching once when a young man lost control of himself, pushed at the people in front of him and fell down on his side. His entire leg turned white – a sight I cannot forget. He had disgraced not just himself but his family and community too. Not only that, he had disrupted the ceremony, and this was believed to have endangered everyone present, putting them at the mercy of the goddess. For this, he was hauled straight to the temple and thrashed. Holy water was sprinkled on the wound. He would later have been taken to hospital and, as far as I remember, there was no announcement that he had passed away so he must have survived (by the blessings of the deity).

In those days, firewalking ceremonies took place in most of the estates in the Nilgiri–Wynaad areas including the colourful Ochterlony Valley and the estates around Gudalur. At Prospect, the largest of the Indian tea estates of the Estates and Agency Company, each of the divisions, Lower Prospect, Upper Prospect, Riverside, and Pykara Falls, had their own firewalking. They competed with one another, each wanting to attract more participants and spend more money to increase the scale of festivity.

Most of the participants were from the village of Kollegal. Prospect was situated about 20 miles from Udhagamandalam, (Ootacamund, as it was named by the British, and better known by the affectionate short-form Ooty). Our labour force was primarily from two areas: around Mysore, and a few villages such as Kollegal and Kunigal. Their language was Kannada, but there were clear caste and social distinctions between them. The Mysore lot belonged to an area that was rich in agriculture, blessed by the bounty of the great River Kaveri. This gave them a definite socio–economic advantage. The people of Kollegal in comparison were rustic village folk accustomed to lives of deprivation and hard labour. They could not claim prosperity or culture; their capital was their endurance and physical strength. They had left their homes, but carried their gods with them. Their faith and devotion had nurtured them through times of difficulties, despair, and disease. And the high-risk Kondam was not just a culmination of their faith but a demonstration of their prowess, a fulcrum of prestige.

Over the years, no matter how many times I viewed the firewalking ceremony, it never lost its impact as a morning of mysticism, devotion, and awe; a tremendous superhuman feat. I remember the excitement among the labour force as the event approached, in my first year on Prospect. It was December 1967, I was twenty years old, and had recently joined the estate as Trainee Assistant Manager.

The labour force was constantly buzzing with plans and activities. The maistry – supervisor – Puttusamy glowed with praise for the workers of his village, Kollegal, who had signed up for this year's Kondam. He told me repeatedly about the powers of Mariamman, the temple deity evoked in this ritual, its purity, and the miracles he had seen over the decades he had seen it being performed. I was fascinated.

Puttusamy himself would have come to work on the tea plantations as a boy. Perhaps he had grown up on an estate where his parents were 'labourers'. He would have worked his way up, and as his skills and aptitude grew, he would have been entrusted with increasing responsibilities.

As a supervisor on Prospect, one of his responsibilities was recruitment. When new areas were planted and

ABOVE: THE ESTATE LABOUR AND THEIR FAMILIES WATCH AS THE PREPARATIONS TO RECEIVE THE FIREWALKERS ARE COMPLETED.

BELOW AND FACING PAGE: THE FIREWALKERS PERFORM ESSENTIAL RITES BY THE RIVER AND THEN WALK IN PROCESSION UP THE HILL TO THE BED OF FIRE THAT AWAITS THEM.

Firewalking is largely a male preserve, and the womenfolk
traditionally stand among the audience grimacing, their teeth
etched and disfigured in black, commemorating an era in which
these measures were taken by women to protect themselves
from marauding forces in times of war. Occasionally – very
occasionally – girls walk the fire too. Ravindran remembers a case
in Rockwood, an estate near Gudalur, when a young girl who
had been brought from the village to take care of the manager's
new-born baby successfully completed the Kondam.

All the firewalking photographs in this book are of the ceremony
at Seaforth Estate, and were taken by Carolyn Hollis in 1966
when her husband David was the manager there. Carolyn, who
is the well-known children's writer Carolyn Sloan, wrote about
the event in the 15 March 1967 edition of *Observer* and some of
her descriptions have been used in this text. Her article included
the line: "I have also heard of the case of a Christian missionary
who rushed onto the fire carrying a bible and crying, 'My faith
is as great as yours!' But his faith was different. He spent weeks in
hospital recovering from severe burns."

At the end of the firewalk, the heroes collapse into the open arms
of their waiting relatives and supporters. More bhasmam is spread
on them. Parched, they gulp water down thirstily. Many are still
somewhat dazed and continue to jump up and down and, as the
tempo of the ritual subsides, gradually emerge from their trance.

additional labour was required, he would travel to his village and bring workers from there, generally a group of thirty or forty at a time. He would pay a salary advance to their families, and their careers and livelihood would thereafter be entrusted to him. On the estate, Puttusamy was responsible for their training and their performance – and also for looking after them. He would ensure that they were given suitable accommodation in the compact living quarters provided by the estate which were referred to, perhaps deriving from a British Army usage, as 'lines'. Puttusamy would bring them to the 'muster shed' to register their attendance for work each day, and ensure that all their details were recorded before they were allocated a specific task. These would be referred to when the time came for wages to be paid.

Being responsible for the quality of people he brought, Puttusamy would show them off proudly. He then had to take them to the field and train them on their tasks, supervising their work and ensuring they delivered quality and productivity that would do him proud.

Each maistry had a large circular Salter spring balance with a dial, and this was used to weigh the baskets of tea leaves plucked by each tea-plucker. The maistrys carried the scales hooked onto the back of their coat collars. These coats were an institution too, and the maistrys used them around the year, somewhat like a uniform. They were proper woollen winter coats, invariably grey in colour, once used by the British masters, who had discarded them when they showed signs of wear, or replaced them with new ones. Heaps of them, redolent with the fragrance of their previous owners, were still to be had in second-hand shops in the Ooty market.

The harvest of tea leaves was weighed twice a day in the muster sheds, once before lunch and once at the end of the day's work. The maistry would note each figure in a table in his ledger, against the plucker's name. In the late 1960s, a kilo of rice cost 88p; an acre of land around Naduvattam could be had for Rs500; a sovereign of gold was valued at Rs50; and a plucker – they were mostly women, but there were also a few elderly men – earned Rs2.26p per day. In winter and monsoon, each plucker's leaf harvest would weigh 10 to 12kg. High season was April-May and September-October, and a plucker could bring in as much as 30 to 40kg. Above 12kg of green leaf weight in a day from a single plucker was awarded with an incentive called 'overweight' of 10p per kg.

The figures were recorded on the check-roll by the assistant field conductor, and at the end of the month, the check-roll clerk would compute salaries. An advance called vatte panam – literally 'cash for the belly' – was issued on Thursdays or Fridays, and the remainder would be disbursed on the 7th of each month. Cash was brought a day before salary day by managerial personnel in their cars from the bank where the estate had an account, stored in estate safes, and disbursed only by the managers.

One summer vacation, my children were joined by their cousins and a group of six of them, aged between seven and ten, set out in the hot afternoon sun. At the end of four hours of toil, they came home with just about 1kg of plucked leaf between them, a life lesson that stayed with them. But this was many years later, long after I had settled into my working life and become a seasoned member of the tea-planting community, generally referred to with respect, and sometimes with envy, as 'planters'.

A fire-walking festival also takes place annually at the Jadayasvámi temple in Jakkanéri under the auspices of a Siváchári Badaga. It seems to have originally had some connection with agricultural prospects, as a young bull is made to go partly across the fire-pit before the other devotees, and the owners of young cows which have had their first calves during the year take precedence of others in the ceremony and bring offerings of milk which are sprinkled over the burning embers.

Kulakambai (the termination -*kambai* denotes a Kurumba village) is for administrative purposes a hamlet of Mélúr, eight miles as the crow flies south-west of Coonoor. It is an important coffee centre, and midway between it and Mélúr, in the valley of the deserted Túdúr village mentioned above (p. 316), is the well-known Terramia tea estate. The falls and hill here have already been mentioned in Chapter I.

Mélúr, a village of 2,947 people, eight miles south-west of Coonoor, is widely known for its fire-walking festival, which is one of the most elaborate on all the plateau. It takes place on the Monday after the March new moon, just before the cultivation season begins, and is attended by Badagas from all over Mérkunád. The inhabitants of certain villages (six in number who are supposed to be the descendants of an early Badaga named Guruvajja, have first, however, to signify through their Gottukárs, or headmen, that the festival may take place; and the Gottukárs choose three, five, or seven men to walk through the fire. On the day appointed the fire is lit by certain Badaga priests and a Kurumba. The men chosen by the Gottukárs then bathe, adorn themselves with sandal, do obeisance to the Udayas of Udayarhatti near Kéti, who are specially invited over and feasted; pour into the adjacent stream milk from cows which have calved for the first time during the year; and, in the afternoon, throw more milk and some flowers from the Mahálingasvámi temple into the fire-pit and then walk across it. Earth is next thrown on the embers and they walk across twice more. A general feast closes the ceremony and next day the first ploughings are done, the Kurumba sowing the first seeds and the priests the next lot.

Finally a net is brought; the priest of the temple, standing over it, puts up prayers for a favourable agricultural season; two fowls are thrown into it and a pretence is made of spearing them; and then it is taken and put across some game path and some wild animal (a sambhar if possible) is driven into it, slain and divided among the villagers. This same custom of annually killing a sambhar is also observed, it may be here noted, at other

A creeper's first foray

Kannan, splendidly clad in the uniform of the Estates and Agency Company, immaculate white trousers and coat with polished brass buttons, was waiting for me when I stepped out of the Blue Mountain Express at Mettupalayam railway station that bright September morning. He courteously helped me into a gleaming black Austin A30 with spotless white cotton upholstery that stood, proud and distinguished, among the other waiting vehicles, the Vauxhalls, Morris Oxfords, and Standard Vanguards, that were used in the Nilgiris in those days. As we started the climb up into the beautiful blue hills which would soon be my home, he blew the horn as we approached blind corners, or to alert an occasional vehicle passing by to give us room to pass. Every time he did so, he would politely say, "Sorry, sir," eyes straight on the road ahead. I would later learn that Kannan had joined the company as a chauffeur many years earlier, bringing with him the discipline and decorum of his army background.

I had visited the Nilgiris for the first time three months previously, arriving in Coonoor by the Nilgiri Mountain Railway to attend an interview. Nervous and self-absorbed, I had remained unaware of my surroundings. Now, the dramatic landscape rose up to claim me, and become my future home. Having grown up in Madras, these surroundings were new and completely unexpected. I certainly knew the sea but had never seen a mountainous jungle before. As we climbed a winding curve up the 30-mile hill road from Mettupalayam to Ooty, I saw a board that said, "Hairpin bend 1/16", and felt perplexed. Wasn't a hairpin that thin, curved metal object that the ladies in my family used to secure coils of their long hair into what we called a bun? Accustomed only to crowded and dusty roads, it was astonishing to me that I was travelling on one lined with trees so thick on either side that light could barely penetrate through them. As the beauty of the environment enveloped me, I felt a rising thrill of adventure and perhaps it was this that protected me from the nausea that the winding road and increasing altitude might have caused a city boy from the plains. When Kannan stopped to fill water from a crystal clear pool, forming as droplets dripped into it from the mossy rocks above, the utter stillness and silence filled me with awe. Gradually, I became aware of a fresh, beautiful fragrance and a loud resonating sound. I would later identify the scent as that of eucalyptus; the sound came from cicadas.

It seemed that we were now about half-way up the mountain. The temperature had dropped, and I found myself feeling cold. A wafting mist engulfed the area and cars that approached could now be seen only because they had turned on their yellow fog lights. For a young man from Madras, this was a strange sensation, akin to climbing into a refrigerator – that new-fangled invention of recent times.

As the Austin A30 continued its climb, it began to drizzle, and then heavy rain began to fall. I had begun to doze and woke abruptly when the car came to a halt. It was nearly dark now, and I could dimly see that a huge tree, a doddamaram – Kannada for 'huge tree'; more commonly known as Australian Blackwood or Accacia Melenoxylon – lay across the road, blocking our entrance into Prospect, where I was to join as a Trainee Assistant Manager. A group of men were crowded around it, two stood and sawed the trunk with cross-cut saws; two sat on their haunches chopping minor twigs with sharp hooked knives; the rest were diligently cutting branches with axes.

It was clear that this operation was going to take several hours; in the years ahead I would learn that a tree of that size could take three or four days to clear. Travelling from one place to another during this season would invariably mean many such delays, as the roads through the hills during the monsoon would always be strewn with trees blocking traffic.

Kannan reversed the car by a few metres, out of the private road that led into Prospect. Instead, he turned left at the fork and we proceeded along the main public road, driving all the way around, through the adjacent Liddellsdale Estate, also one of the properties belonging to the company I was on my way to join, until we had reached our destination.

21

Knocking on a stranger's door

At my interview in Coonoor, one of the questions I had been asked was to describe Naduvattam, the hamlet town closest to Prospect Estate, where I was being considered for a management position. Looking around me now, I felt embarrassed at the answer I had given. I had imagined Naduvattam to be a typical Indian village, the kind of which I had seen many in Kerala and Tamilnadu. I knew that Naduvattam had a post office, and that it had a telephone exchange. But how could I have described an environment which I had never seen before and could not even have imagined?

I had been interviewed by Hugh Jackson, Managing Director of Matheson Bosanquet, an agency that managed several plantations. These included those owned by the company I had applied to, E&A, the Estates and Agency Company, which had four estates in South India, Dunsinane Estate in Ceylon and NDU Estate in Federal Republic of Cameroon. I would later learn that Mr Jackson was a hero of the Royal Air Force, a fighter pilot in the Battle of Britain during the Second World War.

In those days, applicants to a management position were considered only if they came from educated families belonging to a certain socio-economic class, and for this a reference from a well-known or highly-placed person was essential. For a position in the plantation industry, a recommendation was even more important as its managers would be left in complete charge and the company was answerable under the Industrial Disputes Act for decisions pertaining to the wellbeing and employment of members of the labour force.

I had been referred by Govind Swaminadhan, later Solicitor General of the Madras High Court. My father was a senior police officer and they frequently faced each other in court, and had over the years developed a mutual liking and respect.

Mr Jackson asked me why I was considering a job in the plantations instead of taking the scholarship I had been offered by Patrice Lumumba University in Moscow. I replied that I came from a large and close-knit family, it was important for me to start working and earning, and I would have to leave my education incomplete. In that case, he asked, why had I applied for a scholarship at all? I explained to Mr Jackson that I was very interested in plant and marine life and had wished to do research on alternate forms of protein such as krill, which in those days were seen as a possible solution to the global problem of malnutrition following the two world wars. However, when the time came to accept the offer from Russia, I felt constrained by my family responsibilities. With my

MATHESON, BOSANQUET & CO. PRIVATE LTD.

Coonoor

Cochin & Willingdon Island

GRAMS: 'MATHESONS' Inland
'AGENCY' Overseas

GRAMS: 'AGENCY'

PHONE: 2207 TRAVEL DEPT.
2208 GENERAL OFFICE

PHONE: 260
486

P. O. Box No. 1

P. O. Box No. 26

ESTATE AGENTS, PRODUCE MERCHANTS, SUPPLIERS OF TEA CHESTS AND ESTATE REQUIREMENTS, TEA BUYERS, SHIPPERS

AGENTS FOR

The Estates & Agency Co., Ltd.
Craigmore Land & Produce Co., Ltd.
The Parkside (Neilgherry Hills) Estate Co., Ltd.
The Lucky Valley (Nilgiri Hills) Tea Estates, Ltd.
The Miraflores Estates Private Ltd.
The Wallwood Plantations & Agency Private Ltd.
The Commercial Union Assurance Co., Ltd.
The Gresham Life Assurance Society, Ltd.

SECRETARIES FOR

The Coonoor Tea Estates Co., Ltd.
Kaimabetta Estate.
Grove & Bajiecollie Estates.
Peremboocolly Estate.
Greeofield Estate.
Dalquarren Estate.
Walker & Greig (Coonoor) Private Ltd.

AIR   PASSENGER BOOKING AGENTS   SEA

TO ALL COUNTRIES   (Approved by I.A.T.A.)   TO U.K., U.S.A. AND
                                                   CONTINENTAL PORTS

AIR INDIA INTERNATIONAL
B.O.A.C. — T.W.A.
K.L.M. ROYAL DUTCH AIRLINES
AIR FRANCE
INDIAN AIRLINES CORPORATION
AIR CEYLON AND ALL
   CONNECTED AIRLINES

NEDERLAND LINE ROYAL DUTCH
   MAIL
JAVA BENGAL LINE
JAVA PACIFIC LINE
PRINCE LINE
COMPAGNIE DES MESSAGERIES
   MARTIMES
ROYAL ROTTERDAM LLOYD

ASSOCIATES: London   .. MATHESON & CO., LTD., 3, Lombard St., E.C. 3.
              Colombo   .. BOSANQUET & SKRINE LTD., Chatham St., Fort.
              Calcutta .. MATHESON & CO., LTD., 4, Clive Row.
              Hongkong .. JARDINE MATHESON & CO., LTD., 18, Pedder St.
              Singapore .. HENRY WAUGH & CO., LTD., 2, Cecil St.

THIS ADVERTISEMENT, AND THE ADVERTISEMENTS ON PAGES 32, 82, 92, 94, 96, 100, 140, 142, 144, 208, 221, 226, 229, 257, ARE REPRODUCED FROM *PLANTING DIRECTORY OF SOUTHERN INDIA*, COMPILED BY THE SECRETARY, UPASI, COONOOR (1956), WITH KIND PERMISSION FROM UPASI UNITED PLANTERS' ASSOCIATION OF SOUTH INDIA.

senior position in the National Cadet Corps (NCC), the army would have been a natural choice, but my parents wished for a less risk-prone life for me, if possible not too far away from them.

Mr Jackson then grilled me about the NCC and my role in it and, learning that I held the rank of Regimental Quartermaster Sergeant, to which around forty college NCC units of Madras University reported, he seemed convinced that I would be capable of managing the labour force on a tea estate. Mr Jackson and I talked for a while and somehow the conversation turned to a common acquaintance, Mr VK Nair, who was head of the operations of the Brooke Bond Tea Company in Coimbatore, and previously head of Brooke Bond in Burma. When the Japanese invaded during the war, he and his family and staff escaped, walking all the way from Rangoon to Calcutta. Mr Jackson told me that when VK Nair arrived in Calcutta, he submitted to the Brooke Bond office all the company records from Burma, which he had carried all the way despite having fled on foot and had been deeply appreciated for having served the company beyond the call of duty. When I told Mr Jackson that VK Nair was my father's brother, I was gratified to see that he was solemnly impressed. He told me that they had known each other well and, besides their interactions in the course of work, had enjoyed playing tennis together.

And so it was that on 2 September 1967, I found myself at the bungalow of the assistant factory manager of Prospect Estate, KS Medappa, a senior colleague who would be, perhaps unwittingly, my guide and mentor for the next few months.

A BRAND NEW REPUBLIC

In 1967, India was a young nation, freed from colonial rule just twenty years earlier.

The heady fervour when India celebrated independence from British rule soon evolved into the stark facing of a grim reality. Life expectancy was just thirty-two; only two out of ten Indians had the ability to write a letter and read the reply. Such a large percentage of people lived below the poverty line that hunger and malnutrition were commonplace. Along with Independence came Partition, the carving out of a new nation, Pakistan, from India, and this led to the permanent displacement of a vast population from their ancestral homeland, accompanied by large-scale loss of life and property. Many families were separated, and many were ruined in different ways. As a semblance of normalcy was restored and as attempts were made towards economic progress, hostilities broke out again: a sadly depleting Chinese aggression in 1962, followed by war with Pakistan in 1965. The youth of India was anxious and angry. What sort of future lay in store?

It so happened that 1967 provided a small window of opportunity. At Independence, India was a poor country, its resources ravaged by the British Empire, the wars it had fought, and the traumatic separation of the country into two. In an era of fixed exchange rates, the shortage of foreign exchange in India had escalated into a crisis.

The Indian government consequently continued to raise import duties, and over time prohibited the imports of various items. After nineteen years of struggling to cope with the economic implications, India faced its first currency devaluation. Its immediate casualties were the British expatriates.

It was the British who had started the tea industry in India, with the earliest initiatives commencing in the mid-1830s. They were still running the show, but with the rupee drastically devalued against their native currency, it was no longer attractive to them to be earning in rupees. The exodus began. The Prospect manager, Bill Brown, resigned and, shortly afterwards, his replacement David Hollis, the manager of Seaforth Estate, resigned too. In 1968, an Indian manager, Bob Savur, from High Forest Estate in the Anamallais, was promoted to the prestigious position. The company's board of directors was still mostly British, and Mathesons continued to have several British managers, but it was clear that an era was ending. There was some concern in the planter community, and in particular amongst the labour force, about whether the standards and processes set by the representatives of the British Empire would be met by natives. The future seemed uncertain, now that the differentiating factors of colour, language, and royal mandate had been withdrawn, and the plantations would be run under democratic rule.

As history shows, we did run a very healthy industry for the next fifty years, honouring and implementing the beautifully articulated and sensible Industrial Disputes Act, 1947, the Factories Act, 1948, and the Plantation Labour Act, 1951, under which all workers had equal rights.

FAREWELL ADDRESS

Presented to

C. D. HOLLIS, Esq.,

on the eve of his departure from Seaforth Estate

DEAR SIR,

It is with a deep and sincere feeling of sorrow that we have assembled here today to bid you farewell. Indeed the occasion is a sad one, as we have to part with a gentleman, for whom we have the highest feelings of regard and affection, and hence parting is naturally bitter.

During the period of your service on this Estate at different times, you have discharged your duties most sincerely and benevolently, and combined with tact and generosity, you have upheld the prestige and integrity of your office as Manager of this Establishment. It was during your period the record crop of more than a million pounds of tea were harvested on Seaforth last year. It will not be a flattery if we mention that you have exhibited great and noble qualities during the tenure of your office here.

We are sorry to miss Mrs. Hollis and children today on this occasion here and we would request you to convey our affectionate regards to them.

Whilst expressing our heartfelt thanks and sincere gratitude, we do hope, that wherever you go, you will carry with you happy memories of the time you spent in our midst.

With heavy hearts we now bid you farewell and wish you and your family health, long life and happiness. We pray that God Almighty will shower upon you his choicest blessings in the years to come.

We remain,
Yours faithfully,
STAFF OF SEAFORTH.

SEAFORTH ESTATE, }
23rd July 1968. }

Geetha Power Printing Press Mysore.

IMAGE COURTESY CAROLYN HOLLIS

One of the interesting historical offshoots of this transitional period was the reign of the 'brown sahibs', Indians who stepped in to the methods and lifestyle of the departing British. We dressed and ate the way they did, attempted to follow many of their habits that were perceived as upper-class, and were considered – by ourselves and by others – as a superior breed. The labour called us 'dorai' which means 'master'; official letters added 'Esquire', abbreviated Esq., after our names, a word which indicated a superior social standing.

While the label 'brown sahib' is not always considered a complimentary one, it must be said that much of what we inherited was solid, value-based, and stood us in good stead. I remember in particular the volume of Rutherford's Manual, a thick book covered in red calico binding with the word Rutherford written in a large font across the front cover: a symbol of the old world, as it were. A handyman's guide with tips for construction and maintenance, it had invaluable advice on agriculture, pest management, and other issues of core importance to the planter. It was kept on a shelf of the Prospect manager's office, and could be referred to from there, but was far too precious for borrowing to be permitted.

THE CREEPER TAKES ROOT

For my first three months as Trainee Assistant Manager at Prospect, I was referred to by the management as a 'creeper' – in plantation terminology, one that needs to be guided carefully until it begins to bear fruit. Accordingly, I was made a charge of the assistant factory manager, and my home for that duration would be his bungalow in the Lower Prospect division. I was fortunate to be in the care of KS Medappa, who had come to the Nilgiris with planting experience from New Ambady Estate in Kanyakumari district of Tamil Nadu. Under his influence, the creeper would acquire certain skills essential to plantation life.

This included the way I spoke, the way I dressed, and my table manners, and this learning from him, as a role model, has lasted me all my life. At breakfast on my first morning, I started eating my upma the way everyone I had ever known ate it – with my fingers. When I noticed Medu eating with a fork, however, I felt obliged to follow suit. At dinners with other managers, we were served steaks, pies, roast chicken, and other dishes which required the skilful use of cutlery, and I gradually learnt how it was done. No meal was complete without pudding and our butler Lucas, a young man from Kanyakumari, was an expert. He was also charged with the maintenance of the beautiful period bungalow with its shining red floors, polished brass knobs, and sprawling garden. I still remember the way those floors were polished with red cardinal polish, using a half-coconut shell as a handle, and using its fibre to scrub continuously until the floors gleamed like mirrors. Some areas of the living room and dining room were carpeted and the furniture was made of solid teak or rosewood, beautifully-made pieces crafted by master carpenters from Kerala.

One of the peculiar things I had to get used to were the bathrooms. In those days, an Indian bathroom was typically an empty room with a tap used to fill a bucket, from which you poured water on yourself with a mug. Since I had never known it to be anything but warm all year round, water for bathing had always been cold. In the plantation bungalows, however, temperatures were much lower. The bathrooms contained a large enamel-coated metallic tub, a receptacle in which hot water was filled, and you were expected to climb in and lie down as a means to having a bath.

It took some time to get used to this but then of course a time came when it had become not just a natural way to take a bath but also enjoyable. I think this must have coincided with the end of the excruciating loneliness and homesickness I had suffered as I adapted to this new way of life, new surroundings and a climate different to what I had ever experienced before. It was a very difficult phase and I'll always be grateful for the wisdom that had placed me under the companionship and care of an extremely good person; many have been known to flee from plantation life or be driven to alcohol by the stark stillness and isolation.

Prospect, in those days, had one of the most prestigious factories in South India. The estate was at a high altitude

The New
STANDARD
VANGUARD III

The new Standard Vanguard III is not only good to look at —
a car you'll be proud to park anywhere, against the world's
best - but it also provides a completely new conception of
luxury motoring. All the seats are within the wheel base,
ensuring maximum comfort. A large, deep rear boot will take
all the luggage you need.

The 2-litre engine which powers the new Vanguard III is the
latest power unit to come from a Company, world-famous
for its outstanding engineering achievements.

Standard designers and engineers have worked together to provide the driver and passengers of the
Vanguard III with every possible up-to-date refine-
ment to ensure comfortable and safe motoring.

IT makes history

THE UNION CO. (MOTORS) PRIVATE LTD.
MADRAS * BANGALORE * OOTACAMUND

MZ27S-

BESIDES THE STANDARD VANGUARD AND THE AUSTIN A30, THE
STUDEBAKER AND HILLMAN WERE ALSO POPULAR CARS IN THE
NILGIRIS IN THOSE DAYS. TAXIS WERE GENERALLY VAUXHALLS, HARDY
VEHICLES THAT ADAPTED WELL TO THE ROUGH HILLY TERRAIN AND
COULD SQUEEZE IN FAIRLY LARGE FAMILIES.

FROM *PLANTING DIRECTORY OF SOUTHERN INDIA*, UPASI, COONOOR (1956)

and its speciality was the small, narrow-leaved 'China' variety of tea which produced teas of delicate fragrance, or what tea brokers call 'nose'. Though low in yield, the China variety produced teas of superior flavour, coveted by the export market, particularly the United Kingdom.

Peter Sausman was Acting Manager of Prospect, and one day we had an official visit by the Plantation Inspector, Mada Gowda. It was a solemn visit, as plantation inspectors were vested with the powers to take up legal action against managers who did not comply with the provisions of the powerful Plantation Labour Act. Gowda's black and yellow taxi, an old Standard Vanguard, chugged up the steep climb to West Downs bungalow, the residence of the Prospect manager. Peter had asked me to be present at the meeting with Gowda, with whom he was on good terms, and I was formally introduced as the new assistant manager. Gowda, dressed in trousers, woollen coat and a muffler coiled around his neck, spoke self-importantly about the vast jurisdiction over which he wielded extensive powers.

Peter had arranged for tea for the three of us, which the butler brought in a complete tea service: bone-china cups, a teapot covered with a tea cosy, a milk jug, a sugar pot, a silver strainer, and teaspoons.

Peter was a prankster. He knew that Gowda was used to being served tea in a cup, ready to drink, and that, despite all his extensive powers over tea estates, he was unfamiliar with the traditional British way of serving and drinking tea. He genially encouraged Gowda to help himself to a nice hot cuppa. Gowda picked up the teapot nervously and slowly tilted it, directing the spout to his cup. With only half the pot full, no liquid emerged. Seeing this, Peter called out sneeringly, "Put the bloody thing down, man, you haven't squeezed the damn thing enough!" Poor Gowda, with all the wind taken out of his sails, began agitatedly pumping the tea cosy, hoping to coax tea out of the grudging pot. I found Peter's guffaws confusing but did enjoy the super cup of high-grown Prospect tea he proceeded to serve us with, accompanied by homemade tea biscuits.

As a creeper, I rode my motorcycle, a red Jawa, around the tea fields while my bungalow-mate rode his British-built AJS Matchless 350cc to the factory. The labour force on the plantations followed a gender divide. The tea-pluckers were women, and they carried large eeta – reed baskets – on their backs, filling them with shoots they picked from what planters call the 'plucking table', generally with an unopened bud at the top and three leaves below it.

Men carried out tasks such as clearing and planting new fields, and pruning the bushes that had become unproductive. Tea bushes are retained at a height at which plucking is easily carried out by pruning them every five years, resulting in 20 percent of the fields being pruned every year. Weeding was another labour-intensive activity in which unwanted plants were uprooted with a pronged fork, heaped together and removed to unproductive land. Other than copper-based and nickel-based fungicides, the use of chemicals against weeds and to protect the crop from devastating diseases was still quite rare. Factory roofs were invariably sheets of zinc or tin, and supported by wooden purlins and rafters. These were a fire hazard, and the factories were installed with Mather and Platt sprinklers. Most of the original machinery was from the industrial cities of the UK such as Belfast, Birmingham and Glasgow.

Tea manufacture, the method of processing fresh green tea leaves to a stage where they can be stored for use, begins with withering. The leaves, plucked by hand, would be laid out on the top floors of the factory in jute hessian blinds, strung in several layers on wooden frames. Some skill was required to direct the natural flow of wind to help the leaves to wither, and this activity was directed by the person in charge of production, called the 'teamaker'. The next stage, when the leaves were sufficiently withered, invariably began in the early hours of morning. One test was to pick up a bunch and roll it in your hands. If the leaves clung together and formed a ball which, when thrown in the air, retained its shape, they were considered ready for the rollers.

As the withered leaves were crushed, their natural oils were released and the fragrance rose out of the factory windows and mingled with the mist that sat lightly on its roof of corrugated tin sheets, wafting across the estate and for miles around, a heady signature aroma that pervaded the atmosphere in which the tea planters and their families lived.

WOODBROOK

I woke early one morning a few days ago, with a shrill, persistent call sounding in my ear: "Oodabrukk! Oodabrukk!" It was such a lifelike rendering of the bus conductor calling out to wake dozing passengers to disembark at Woodbrook, that I awoke swamped in nostalgia for a time I had left behind more than fifty years ago.

In those days, and perhaps even today, the Gudalur–Ooty bus stopped at a sharp turn on the Naduvattam road where the path that led up the hill to Woodbrook started. Waiting passengers would push their way in, as stragglers raced frantically down the hill to join them – in those days there were only two buses a day between Ooty and Gudalur. These carried not just passengers but also mail bags with letters and money orders – a postal service by which economic migrants who lived away from their families sent money home – and also provisions from the plains for those who lived in the remote hills. In fact, it was this bus that brought Firdous Darashah's rations – including eggs, rice and tomatoes. Firdous's father Safi, a popular and well-known cricketer, worked as Secretary in the court of the Maharaja of Mysore, and they were sent for him from the palace. Around the bend, the road forked and up the hill was the Woodbrook bungalow, my first independent home, which I shared with Firdous for the few months of his plantation career.

Woodbrook nestled in a lush wooded area and, unbelievably, had an actual brook running right through it. Culverts had been built at the points where it entered and exited the bungalow; it flowed under a fence and continued its downhill journey, feeding into a rivulet below. Small cobblestones had been placed at intervals in the house too. During the monsoon its level rose, and in places small ponds appeared.

Woodbrook was originally an independent estate owned by an individual proprietor and, possibly at some time in the 1940s, was acquired by E&A as a division of Prospect. Woodbrook lay on a hillside and, perhaps because it was owned by an individual without the resources of a company, the bungalow, which had been built in the late 19th century, fitted the contours of the hill. To reach the kitchen, a small knoll had to be navigated and at night, when it was quite often pitch dark, the staff, such as the bearers who carried crockery and cutlery back and forth, needed a certain degree of skill.

Woodbrook had no electric supply, and the garage housed a Lister Blackstone Engine which was cranked to start every evening as the sun went down and provided electricity to the bungalow for three or four hours after which, on a moonless night, it would be pitch dark. Occasionally an owl picking out beetles or insects in the firewood shed would hoot, or the silence would be broken by the shrill mating or flight calls of a deer. Sometimes the howling wind knocked against ancient windowpanes, and though you knew it was impossible, it did sound as if an unearthly creature was trying to get in. And once, just as the witching hour struck, I woke to the sound of loud human moans from outside the open window next to my bed. I don't need to explain that the old plantation bungalows had no bars on their windows; nor do I need to describe the kind of courage I had to muster, all alone at night, to lean out and look around! There, under the window lay an unknown person shrouded in a cumblie – a field blanket, an item that every worker in the estate was issued and often wore right through the day and night. I called out loudly, asking who it was and what they wanted. The moaning continued unabated. In a state of fear, I slipped out of the bungalow on my bike and returned with maistry Moodligiri. The man lying curled up in his cumblie outside my window turned out to be one of the crèche cook Chinnappan's twin sons. He was mentally challenged, and I was informed that he was often turned out of his home at night by thugs so that they could have his wife to themselves. It turned out that the man was hungry so we gave him a good meal and the maistry then escorted him home. Such incidents, I must clarify, were very rare. Most of the time we were surrounded by peace, stillness and complete silence.

My closest neighbour, V Ramaswamy, lived 3 miles away, in the TR Bazaar bungalow. Barring a patch of tea on one side, Woodbrook was completely surrounded by wattle, rhododendron and eucalyptus trees. Damp leaves layered a woodland floor rich with algae, moss, fern and lichen. The shola – grove – was home to hare, mouse deer, flocks of brown woodcock and brightly plumaged jungle fowl. The latter was a noisy creature and I often woke to its sharp clucks. In the early months of the year, swarms of honey bees, butterflies and dragonflies flocked around the blooms of Calendula, Chrysanthemum and Saponaria slurping their nectar quite oblivious of my presence in the garden. With the advent of the monsoon, the brook of Woodbrook drew larger visitors like Barking Deer and Nilgiri Tahr.

On the slope below stood two make-shift sheds with heaps of eucalyptus leaves piled around them. They contained crude stills and when these were fired, wisps of smoke wafted idly out, and the lightest breeze would spread the fragrance of freshly-distilled eucalyptus oil all around.

The road up the hill to Woodbrook was steep and slippery. It was paved with roughly-hewn granite stones cobbled decades ago, perhaps for the horses of a phaeton to trot uphill. One foggy night, rather than relying on its single-candle power headlight, I abandoned my beloved red Jawa at the bottom of the hill and began the trudge home in total darkness. I slipped and fell into what I thought was a small ditch. When I reached the bungalow, I was horrified to see, under the light of a hurricane lantern, that there was blood all over my hands and body! Had I been much more badly hurt in the fall than I had realised? And if so, why was I not in any pain? Next morning, the mystery was solved. What I had fallen into was the carcass of a cow that had evidently been killed by a panther.

Another time, I set out from home wearing my large canvas raincoat, led my Jawa to the edge of the slope, sat on it and allowed it to start rolling down. Those bikes often needed to be kickstarted and in the monsoon, as the humidity continued to rise, quite often even a few kicks would not suffice. As the bike picked up speed, I pressed the lever to engage a gear, and jerked my foot off the clutch. The engine started – but a sudden movement

MESSRS MATHESON, BOSANQUET & CO., LTD.

POST BOX NO. 1. COONOOR-1 (S. INDIA)

TELEPHONE: 2207
TELEGRAMS: AGENCY

<u>Registered</u>.

REGISTERED OFFICE:
BELMONT, COONOOR-1.
NILGIRIS. (S. INDIA)

TD- A/8/483/69.

3rd March, 1969.

The Manager,
Prospect Estate,
Prospect Estate P.O.,
Nilgiris.

Dear Sir,

<u>Mr. M. Ravindran.</u>

With reference to our telephone conversation of last week, we have pleasure in enclosing herewith Mr. Ravindran's air ticket from Coimbatore to Madras on 8th March and return on 7th April 1969. We have debited this account with a sum of Rs. 243/- through the Estate Memo.

The flight timings are as follows:-

8-3-69	Report at Coimbatore Peelamedu Airport		12 15
	IC-542 Coimbatore	d	12 45
	Madras	a	14 05
7-4-69	IC-541 Madras	d	08 50
	Coimbatore	a	10 10

Kindly acknowledge receipt of the enclosure.

Yours faithfully,
Per Pro M/s Matheson Bosanquet & Co., Ltd.

IATA

Branch: ORIENTAL BUILDING, OOTACAMUND. Phone: 604.

against my leg alarmed me. I saw with a shock that it was a rat snake, and, leaping off the bike, stood and watched it roll down the slope without a rider while the snake slithered off.

Despite the proximity of panther and snake, my memories of Woodbrook are filled with warmth and nostalgia. The end of this first phase of my new life was marked by my furlough – a leave of absence granted to members of certain professions such as planters, civil servants and missionaries. I packed my bags, delighted at the prospect of being with my family again. Matheson's travel division booked my air ticket (at more than double the price of a first-class train ticket). Once again I sat in the back seat of the gleaming black Austin A30 and Kannan drove me to Coimbatore airport. As per his orders, he drove the car onto the tarmac, stopping when he reached the single aircraft that stood on the runway – a French-made Caravelle jet plane, one of the earliest jets used for civil aviation – which waited there with its door open. I had inherited a privilege provided to covenanted executives who were British subjects and entitled to the assurance of a safe passage on their way 'home'; Kannan was responsible for my safety and he accordingly handed me over to the pilot and, with a smart salute, turned around and got back into the car and began the long journey back up into the blue hills.

THE GUM TREE AND THE FOREST

Excerpted from *Southern India* painted by Lady Lawley and described by F.E. Penny, published by A.&C. Black London, October (1914) p210-213.

The hill tribes are of no use in the gardens of Ootacamund and Coonoor. They can fell trees and cut down jungle ; perhaps put up a garden fence ; but there their utility ends, and the lover of flowers must look to another race to tend his roses and picotees, his geraniums and heliotrope, his dahlias and tuberoses. The Canarese, the agriculturist of Mysore and the plateaus of the Western Ghat, is the man he must turn to for the care of his flowerbeds. The work of weeding and watering is congenial to the Canarese, and both men and women follow the calling of Adam con amore.

The old woman with the basket on her head has spent the whole of her life among the flowers in the Government House gardens at Ootacamund. In her indigo sari, with its broad border of yellow green, she is in colour harmony with the mimosa that scents the air. Like one of the creatures of the forest she moves noiselessly and goes through her task without haste, cleaning paths, weeding beds and borders, removing dead leaves and sticks and tidying up after the pruner. She is in keeping with the green barbets and grey babblers that haunt the grevillea trees and rose hedges, and with the green and black butterflies and metallic honey-suckers that rob the fuchsia bells.

The mimosa was introduced with the eucalyptus from Australia in the middle of the nineteenth century, and it flourishes exceedingly, bidding fair to become a pest like the lantana. A Revenue Official of the Nilgiris named Thomas planted numbers of blue gums as well as black gums (the Acacia melanoxylon) and the wattle. The gums have grown into large forest trees, and they have given Ootacamund the appearance of having been built in a forest. When the place was first opened up by Sullivan the site was little better than a bog. It was bare of trees except for small sholas in the moist valleys. Now the place is thickly wooded with the evergreen gum.

The eucalyptus and the melanoxylon have a sombre and distinct beauty of their own ; the one a dark heavy green, the other almost grey in the brilliant sunlight. In its early growth the eucalyptus clothes itself in a tender foliage of emerald bloom. When it reaches maturity it loses the round leaf and assumes a tough scimitar-shaped foliage not unlike that of the English willow. The trunk, tall and straight, sheds its bark in long ragged streamers that sway in the wind and give the tree an appearance of decay it is far from experiencing. Wood, bark, seeds, and foliage are strongly impregnated with the pungent oil which is now an article of commerce in South India. Neither fern nor shrub will grow beneath the tree, a fact that alters the character of the eucalyptus forest and makes it entirely different from the indigenous sholas.

The native calls it the firewood tree, as every part of it will burn green. The frayed ribbons of bark constantly falling from its stem, together with the dry leathery leaves, form a perennial harvest to the wood-gatherer.

THE PLANTER'S LIFE

Excerpted from *The Wynaad and The Planting Industry of Southern India*, **by Francis Ford, Madras (1895) p18**

The planter's life in the Wynaad is healthy, free and open. For a youngster, who is fond of active pursuits but unaccustomed to menial drudgery, there is no profession like it. It has all the charm and none of the hardship of the American ranches or Australian sheep-farm. The planter has at his beck and call domestic servants ; he is within easy reach of markets where good fresh meat is obtainable ; he can grow his own vegetables, and so far as diet is concerned, he gets much the same food with as little trouble to himself as he did in England. Of course the quality of the beef and mutton of an Indian bazaar is not as high as that to be bought from a West End butcher, but it is on the whole very fair. A great advantage are the domestic servants. Within doors the planter is as carefully looked after as ever in his life, and, should he determine to marry, he can bring his wife to a home where she will take command of a household, and not be herself that household all in one - cook, housemaid, parlourmaid and mistress - with none to help in the wearying duties but an uppish hired girl.

The plantation bag

The foundation of India's tea industry was laid by the expatriate British, and many of our early practices, from management methods to social rituals, were inherited from them. One of these was the tradition of the plantation bag: a bag of goodies that would arrive on the estate periodically. This was a large leather bag filled with goodies from England which were coveted by planters with longing for special treats from 'back home', a phrase frequently used by expatriate British when they referred to England, or 'Blighty' as they sometimes called it. These included items such as cheese, chocolates and cosmetics, still quite rare in India at the time. The bags were packed at the company's London Wall office and came by ship from Southampton to Madras Port, where they would make their way to the Coonoor Post Office. In return, the estates sent the finest leaf tea packed in specially made 5kg wooden chests. The regular size for trade was 50kg, but these smaller boxes were sent as exclusive gifts to the owners, stencilled with the estate name, specially picked and winnowed with every trace of fibre removed, and personally packed by the manager or assistant. These the owners would keep for their own enjoyment, while also gifting some boxes to members of the church and the royal family.

By the time I joined plantation life, the plantation bag had long been made redundant. However, one of its most prized contents continued to be sent to us at intervals: a month's collection of the Daily Telegraph. Each newspaper was folded into a light blue sleeve and I still remember the feel of those crisp pages, as fine as the skin of an onion. Considering the length of the sea journey, by the time we received them the news would already be more than a month old. Still, they were valuable to us and read carefully because they immersed us in another world and gave us exposure not just to the outdated happenings of another place but also to language, editorial analysis and the cultural norms to which we aspired. Reading these papers gave us information about events in the British Parliament and the Church of England. I would not be exaggerating if I said that the Daily Telegraph would play a significant role in determining the course of my career! This happened with the visit of our company's chairman, Sir John Arbuthnot, in the year 1969.

Sir John (1912-1992) was educated at Eton and Cambridge, receiving his MA in 1938. In the Second World War he rose to the rank of Major in the Royal Artillery. Sir John's father, Major Kenneth Wyndham Arbuthnot, had served in the North West Frontier of India as well as in Africa and was killed in action when his son was three years old. His regiment for twenty-two years was Seaforth Highlanders – and I have always wondered whether this was where the name of Seaforth Estate was derived from. Major Kenneth's father, William Reirson Arbuthnot (1826-1913), was a British businessman and legislator highly placed in the banking industry in Madras, member of the Madras Legislative Council, and listed as the proprietor of Prospect Estate on page 197 of the Nilgiri Guide and Directory by JSC Eagan, 1916.

A VISIT FROM SIR JOHN

A full month before our chairman's visit, the office received a letter in the post with his detailed itinerary which, I believe, would have been dictated by the chairman to his secretary, who would have taken notes in shorthand before typing it up, making corrections as per his instructions, perhaps more than once, and sending it off. From 8am to 5pm, the chairman would visit the factories of each of the estates, tour the fields in the Austin A30, and inspect the labour lines and other facilities provided by the company such as schools, dispensary, canteens and provision stores. An important part of the itinerary was a detailed menu which was to be prepared for each of his meals, detailing items like shrimp cocktail and pink gin, which was our chairman's drink. He would carry his own bottle of the finest British-made gin, and I remember the ceremony with which a few drops of Angostura Bitters would be spun around to coat the inside of a goblet after which the gin was carefully poured in to uniformly absorb the flavour and light pink hue. The menu, of course, was a nightmare for Situ, the manager's wife, who would be in a state of high anxiety which rose as the big day approached!

I remember the conversation over drinks at West Downs, which preceded a grand formal dinner held for the chairman, with the senior executives of E&A hanging on to his every word. Our chairman, a portly gent in his fifties, was an amiable, charming and reassuring man. A seasoned British politician, he stayed firmly away from topics such as politics and religion, and stuck to uncontroversial subjects such as the weather. Over the years, I would learn how blessed we in India are, with stable climate within each season, while in England the as-yet unpredictable variations from day to day made it difficult to plan even the simplest picnic. That evening, Sir John told us about the traffic jams in London which were due not just to fog but a new element, smog, which had created national panic since its first major occurrence in December 1952. Sir John had been instrumental in framing the Clean Air Acts of 1956 and 1968, and spoke passionately about this and other neutral subjects. When asked a question, he would pause and think, and answer carefully and with courtesy. He also made an effort to speak to each of us individually, and this is where I was pleased with my studious perusal of the Daily Telegraph as I was able to stand my ground quite well.

V RAMASWAMY, BOB SAVUR, SIR JOHN ARBUTHNOT, LS KUMAR AND VICTOR DEY AT BELLE VUE DIVISION, LIDDELLSDALE

IMAGE COURTESY P PATRICK OF BELLEVUE SCHOOL. FROM SAAZ'S ALBUM

At the grand dinner, as we sat down around the gleaming rosewood table of the West Downs dining room, I will admit that my appetite was somewhat restrained by the extended stretch of unusually good behaviour. So it was a relief when the irrepressible Peter Sausman announced, "Please pass the butter. All my cream for the last two weeks went into it!" We assistant managers doubled up in suppressed guffaws at his irreverence, and luckily our chairman did not inquire what he meant; perhaps he had not understood the implication (or perhaps he had!)

Amul and India's dairy revolution had not yet reached our part of the country. Stocks of Polson's butter were irregular in Ooty – which, at a distance of 20 miles, was an hour's drive. There were a few vintage Frigidaires in some of the managers' bungalows, but electricity fluctuated, sometimes absent for hours at a time. Homes were supplied with milk by the owners of cows in the vicinity and we had all been instructed to collect fresh cream and send it to the manager's bungalow. Here it was now, churned into butter to prepare the chairman's meals and served, arranged into stylish curls, on a dish placed on the table – and Peter was claiming his share.

BIRTH OF AN ERECTION ENGINEER

After dinner, we gathered in the smoking room of West Downs and the chairman cordially informed me that he wanted a draft layout of the bungalow and that I would be the perfect person to make one for him. I could show it to him at breakfast next day. The huge colonial bungalow had a complicated plan, with corridors, passages, bay and bow windows, and porticos. Having stayed up half the night struggling with sketches and measurements,

I presented myself once again at West Downs next morning. My manager had a knowing look on his face, and he and the chairman gave a cursory glance to the amateur plan before looking at each other and nodding. They then announced that I was being transferred to the Seaforth factory to help install CTC machines.

I was thrilled. It was a promotion: an acknowledgement of the work I had done, and the potential they saw in me. The Seaforth CTC machines were among the earliest such machines to be installed in South India and I was privileged to have been selected to work there. As a junior planter, most of my work had been outdoor weather-based agricultural activity and supervising labour in the fields. In the factory, an engineering mindset was essential as layouts had to be balanced and geometrically aligned, and various calculations would be required to install and run machinery. Doubtless my sketch of West Downs had conveyed that I was capable of filling the available position.

In those days, Prospect was producing only traditional or 'orthodox' tea — high-grown teas manufactured with an emphasis on preserving their subtle aroma and flavour — and the output was almost entirely exported to the UK. With the new CTC machine, E&A was for the first time exploring the Indian market, producing tea using the Crush-Tear-Curl process which produces a dark, cloudy tea that leaves an astringent aftertaste, and which was becoming increasingly popular in India. It was boiled rather than brewed, and, drunk with copious quantities of milk and sugar, it was seen as a tea for the working classes as it provided nourishment as well as energy. Seaforth Estate was at a lower elevation and produced tea suitable for this process. The manager was NSV Sinniah, an experienced planter who had worked for some years in Ceylon (as Sri Lanka was then known) before coming to the Nilgiris. He was a highly regarded manager, known for his exceptional engineering bent of mind, and it would be a privilege for me to assist him on the shop floor.

With the chairman's visit out of the way and a new assignment to look forward to, my colleagues and I enjoyed an unrestrained celebration, drinking to our brilliant future, and they awarded me with the title Erection Engineer, a label that any young man would be proud of.

8 June 1992 Sir John Arbuthnot, Bt

"Dļelegraph"

SIR JOHN ARBUTHNOT, Bt, the former Conservative MP for Dover, who has died aged 80, was a stern foe of Government profligacy and a pillar of the Anglican laity.

Shortly before he lost his seat in the 1964 general election after 14 years as an MP, Arbuthnot was created a baronet — one of the last Tory backbenchers to be so rewarded.

John Sinclair-Wemyss Arbuthnot was born on Feb 11 1912, the elder son of Major K W Arbuthnot, of the Seaforth Highlanders, who was killed in action at the second Battle of Ypres in 1915. Besides Scots lairds, his ancestors included the colourful figure of Johnnie Fa, the Romanie gypsy recognised by James V as "Lord and Earl of Little Egypt" in 1540.

Young John was educated at Eton and Trinity College, Cambridge. He began his career in 1934 with Estates & Agency Holdings, a firm specialising in Indian tea, which he subsequently chaired. In the same year he also entered politics as the prospective Conservative candidate for the Don Valley division of Yorkshire.

Having stood unsuccessfully in the 1935 election he was adopted for the Dunbartonshire division.

During the Second World War he served with the Royal

Arbuthnot: watchdog

Artillery. He was wounded and attained the rank of major. Afterwards he was selected as Conservative candidate for Dover, but failed to win the seat amid the Labour landslide of 1945. He was victorious five years later and fast established himself as an assiduous constituency MP.

He championed Dover's "three Cs" ("coal, chalk and corn") and worked tirelessly for miners suffering from silicosis and pneumoconiosis, while making a minor reputation as an advocate of reduced government.

From 1952 to 1957 Arbuthnot was parliamentary pri-

vate secretary to a succession of ministers of Pensions and Health. In 1955 he joined the influential Public Accounts Committee, whose purpose, as he put it, "is to make sure the nation is getting value for money".

As a backbench watchdog Arbuthnot was merciless in ferreting out waste. On one occasion his stern questioning revealed that the number of motor-cars in the British Embassy in Paris had leapt from a pre-war level of three to 45.

He was elected to the executive of the 1922 Committee and in 1958 became a member of the Speaker's Panel of temporary chairmen, who chaired debates in the Speaker's absence.

Despite his economic liberalism, Arbuthnot's views on social matters were more interventionist. During the debate on the abolition of capital punishment, he suggested that the perpetrators of serious crimes should be whipped, in addition to any other punishment that might be meted out.

Later he urged the reintroduction of the birch: "I deplore the fact that Parliament has been so weak that a schoolmaster dare not tan little Tommy's backside, without running the risk of parents taking action against him for assault".

He was member of Lord Crathorne's Committee on Sunday Observance, which reviewed the law surrounding sports and pastimes: but when the committee reported its findings in 1964, Arbuthnot dissented from portions of it, arguing that Sunday theatre performances would result in pressure being brought on actors to work against their wishes.

Arbuthnot's stance was influenced by his staunch Low Church Anglicanism. From 1962 to 1964 he was Second Church Estates Commissioner, responsible to parliament for the stipends and pensions of the clergy. Arbuthnot went on to become one of the Church Commissioners for England and was appointed chairman of a commission to inquire into the organisation of diocesan boundaries. He was a member of the Church Assembly and the General Synod.

Arbuthnot was appointed MBE in 1944 and awarded the Territorial Decoration in 1951.

He married, in 1943, Jean Duff; they had two sons and three daughters. The elder son, William Reierson Arbuthnot, born 1950, succeeds to the baronetcy. The younger son, James Arbuthnot, is currently Conservative MP for Wanstead and Woodford, and an Assistant Whip.

SIR JOHN OBITUARY IN *DAILY TELEGRAPH* 18 JUNE 1992

posted by Michael Rhodes for *Peerage News* HTTPS://PEERAGENEWS.BLOGSPOT.

COM/2018/08/OBITUARY-SIR-JOHN-ARBUTHNOT-BT-1992.HTML

ABOVE: THE SEAFORTH BUNGALOW SWIMMING POOL.
BELOW: DAVID HOLLIS AT THE HIGH FOREST NURSERY.
ORIGINAL PHOTOGRAPHS BY CAROLYN HOLLIS

REMEMBERING

A note from Carolyn Hollis

In our time, Matheson's consisted of Seymour Molyneux, then Hugh Jackson and then David Hacking. Hugh Jackson, I think he had been a prisoner of war, and I remember being told it showed in some of his nervous habits.

Sir John Arbuthnot and Sidney Bolster came to visit on alternate years, always early in the year when it was cold in England. I liked it when Lady Arbuthnot came too, he was less grand then. Sir John addressed the nursery workers at High Forest as if he was in the Houses of Parliament. David could hardly translate for laughing. I spoke to Lady Arbuthnot some years back, she was living alone in London. She said, "I remember you driving me around the estate with no shoes on in that old land rover." I said, "I remember you taking seasick pills to go on an elephant ride."

It's good to know that the Seaforth pool was still used after we left. David had it built without approval from Mathesons. They were not happy! Bill Brown fell in with all his clothes on one day – he was accident prone.

Peter Sausman – I fear he came to a sad end. He could not come to terms with being Anglo Indian (unlike his brother Colin, manager of Terrace, the last remaining estate owned by the Maharaja of Mysore which bordered Belle Vue.) He was in the Fleet Air Arm during the war, and lost a plane trying to land on an aircraft carrier. He had a photo of the carrier over the mantelpiece at Prospect. We were looking after his imported fox terrier (very spoilt and expensive) while Peter was having his hand treated after he lost a finger in the Prospect Factory. A panther took it off the open veranda when it followed me down to the kitchen one night. Poor Peter.

Leeches! I don't even want to think about them! And I remember the board at the Ooty Club showing MFHs (Master Fox Hounds) of the hunt. On the list of years, hard to miss, "1857 – The Mutiny".

Another memory is of playing tennis with Mrs Veeraraghavan at the Wellington Club, she beat me hollow. I got a women's cricket team together in the Anamallais. The men's captain and second were so disparaging they wouldn't play. Mrs Veeraraghavan was a demon bowler and I seem to remember that we won the match.

THE ANAMALLAI CLUB TENNIS COURT, OVERLOOKING THE CRICKET MATCH PLAYED BETWEEN EXPATRIATE BRITISH AND INDIAN PLANTERS. ORIGINAL PHOTOGRAPH BY CAROLYN HOLLIS

A WORM OF THE HIPPOCRATIC CORPUS

My first friends at Seaforth were the leeches, particularly during the timber operations when we worked with elephants.

The leeches were everywhere. Everyone on the estate – managers, workers, cattle and wild animals – was a host to the leeches. It was impossible to walk in the fields for even a few minutes without having them swarm up your legs. The Nilgiri leeches were much smaller and accordingly milder in comparison to their cousins lower down the hills, which were more like the bloodletting leeches of ancient systems of medicine. These leeches drew blood, sucking it through the interstices of our socks. Because of the cold and damp, we could barely feel them until they fell off, fully fed and satiated. After that, the anti-coagulating enzyme that helps the leech to feed unimpeded remained active for some hours and the bleeding would continue. We would stick stamp-sized bits of newspaper on the wounds as the most effective way to stop the bleeding. As a result, the planter in the fields, wearing shorts and with his knees bare, often formed a ludicrous spectacle, with stamps stuck all over him as if he was some sort of postal article, ready for dispatch. When he stood aside and bent to wrench the suckers out from his body, a few more would climb up across his shoes and embark on the ascent to warmer climes.

The itching of a leech bite continued for days, and if

the scab was disturbed, blood would ooze again. In the evening, sinking into the bathtub for a long, hot soak, the 'stamps' fell off and the bathwater turned pink.

Leeches, it must be said, were fair and liberal in their attack. They would suck blood from a convict just as much as from a policeman. Even the aggressive trade union leader was so tormented by the mighty leech that he was in agreement with the other side at least in the subject of leech bite. In the case of animals with hides, including elephants, the parasite would pick their easy-to-access hoof-dividers as well as tender areas like the nose, mouth and even eyelids. It was a sad sight to see bitten animals trying in vain to get the sucker off their bodies. The worst sufferers were the women workers, many of whom were already anaemic and could ill afford further loss of blood.

Salt is a traditional method which draws water out of the body of some creatures and when dropped on a leech you will see it shrivel up and fall off its victim. However, in the rain or damp, salt is ineffective. One of our daily chores as assistant managers was to issue workers with leech ointment, a preventive concoction of tobacco and oil, to be applied on arms and legs before they went to work. Even then, when rain washed the ointment off, leeches would loop up to hidden parts of the body and have their fill, unhindered.

Leeches survived for millennia with no effective measures to mitigate their attack, but the continuous use of fertilisers, fungicides, pesticides and weedicides to make the ground bare, have reduced their populations significantly in plantations today.

DANCE OF THE ELEPHANT

In the early 1970s, Estates and Agency was taken over by a Kapur family with business interests including hotels in Bombay and tea estates in South India. E&A's holding of Prospect, Liddellsdale, Seaforth and High Forest were expanded to include Nonsuch, Terramia, Bonaccord and Ponmudi. Many significant events occurred following this acquisition, but the one which stands out most vividly in my memory is one in which I learnt that elephants have a sense of humour and will have a good laugh when something funny happens. And, that their cognition is so good that they can even sense a holiday!

I was at Seaforth when its new owners decided to harvest rosewood from the estate's Yellamalai Division. Four of us chinna dorais – Victor, Nana, Cyrus and me, were deputed to supervise the operations. Chinna means 'little' or 'young' in Tamil, and dorai, or 'master' was the word used for the colonial bosses, inherited by Indian managers on the plantations. We were allocated different duties and set to work. Bulldozers, an innovation from the plains, cleared the earth and helped move the logs after they were cut. However, it was a time when technology did not have all the answers. The terrain was such that the traditional method of using elephants to do these tasks was still necessary.

Cyrus was given charge of the timber camp where elephants were picking the logs and placing them on lorries, dispatching them to Cochin from where they would sail across the seas in exchange for substantial gains. One day, as he walked behind his team of three elephants, a mahout warned him in a friendly way that his elephant Fatimakutty happened to be suffering a bout of indigestion. Sure enough, as if to oblige her mahout by supporting his words, Fatimakutty let out a loud rumble, roll and boom that harked of distant thunder, and sprayed poor Cyrus with a blast of hot air and gas. We rocked with guffaws when he later told us about this, and Nana in his inventive way would recount the story of how Fatimakutty had let fly and Cyrus, who had the misfortune of being in its direct path, reeled back spitting bits of bamboo and other semi-digested elephant excrement. He then proceeded to remove his glasses and lo, his face rendered green by Fatimakutty, had two white circles where his glasses had been.

A FESTIVAL ON SEAFORTH WITH CELEBRATIONS AT THE BOTTOM OF
THE DRIVE TO THE MANAGER'S BUNGALOW.
ORIGINAL PHOTOGRAPH BY CAROLYN HOLLIS

So much did we enjoy this latter story that over time it became the official version of what had actually happened. The illusory dung left its residue: even today we debate on what had actually happened to Cyrus, and muse on the pitfalls of walking too close to an elephant.

The first tree that was felled was a magnificent specimen, its roots deep in the verdant valley which had nourished it so well that it had grown and continued to grow until the day when it lay amputated on the ground measuring 20 feet in length and 6 feet in girth. Crowds gathered and watched with awe. A log of that size would entirely occupy a platform lorry, with no space to spare for any other cargo. Whispers circulated furiously, speculating on the value of such an enormous, pristine log of wood. How would it be brought up to the road to be transported out? And then in came Fatimakutty, lumbering along, with her mahout sitting on her back. The log had been prepared with a tiny hole in it and a rope put through and firmly knotted. The other end was thrown up to go over the shoulder of the elephant who would then gradually heave the log up from the valley to the clearing where it could be loaded onto the waiting platform lorry.

The mahout coaxed Fatimakutty to walk, pulling the log along. It was a long struggle, a few inches at a time with intervals of standing still in between. As the intervals grew longer, the frustrated mahout shouted out angrily, demanding that everyone leave. The audience was quickly shooed away, leaving the mahout to do his magic and less than ten minutes later, the log had been hauled up and lay on the clearing.

We later learnt the mahout's secret: a range of coercive

measures to be employed in such circumstances, such as inserting a stick under a toenail – and worse. These he could not have done in front of such a huge crowd and Fatimakutty knew very well that as long as there were people watching, she was safe. And when the crowd left, she knew equally well that if she did not do as ordered, she faced the risk of torture, and quickly complied.

Now as it happens, Yellamalai, which borders on Gudalur, had a large stretch of virgin jungle that extended over more than a thousand acres, the Kathleen Jungle, which had been leased to E&A along with Seaforth by the royal family of Nilambur who, challenging the removal of trees on their property, went to court and obtained a stay order. Thus it was that, one week into the operations, a liveried court Amin – a traditional title given to officials who perform a range of court duties – stepped out of a forest jeep at a clearing in Kathleen.

THE ORIGINAL PHOTOGRAPHS ON PAGES 60, 116, 117, 118, 132, 133, 175, AND 230 ARE BY DR ARULNATHAN, A MEDICAL DOCTOR WITH THE HIGHWAVYS GROUP. THEY REFLECT HIS PASSION FOR NATURE, FOR TRACKING ELEPHANTS, AND FOR WILDLIFE PHOTOGRAPHY, WHICH HE HAS PURSUED FOR MORE THAN FORTY YEARS.

To this day the scene is clearly etched in my mind. The foul smell of beedi smoke hung in the dense misty air. The rain continued to beat down relentlessly, falling on the rosewood too, enhancing the colour of the cut logs to a beautiful, glistening black. The freshly-moved earth was slushy and slippery underfoot and we had to repeatedly bend and pluck fattened leeches from our legs. How wonderful it would have been to have a cup of tea at this moment! Just then, the Amin arrived. Splendidly outfitted in a pure white coat with a blood-red sash on which was pinned a shining brass insignia, he unfurled the decree he had brought with him in grand style and read it aloud, bringing the operation to a grinding halt.

The three elephants somehow understood that the man in the grand uniform had declared a holiday for them. Fatimakutty, Khader and Kannan raised up their front legs and stomped around in a happy dance, trumpeting what were clearly chuckles of glee. And then, to the helpless consternation of their mahouts, they ran off to their camp to relax for the rest of the day. And who could blame them? Nobody ever enjoyed micromanagement and bullying styles of getting work done!

Today Kathleen is a settlement of homes and fields which have been cultivated over the decades to produce spices such as cardamom, ginger and pepper. The historic dance of the elephants, witnessed by four young chinna dorais among a huge crowd of rivetted locals today offers tourists, oblivious to its recent past, an opportunity to enjoy a break from their city lives.

Two leaves and a bud

Two Leaves and a Bud is a novel by Mulk Raj Anand, first published in 1937. Set in the tea plantations of Assam, it is based on the exploitation of the estate's labour force by the British manager. It is the terribly sad story of a peasant who goes to work on a tea estate, having fallen into debt and lost his own lands, promised that he will soon save enough to buy back his land. He soon finds that he has been tricked: he now cannot even afford to feed his family. Worst of all, his wife and daughter are subjected to rape and other sexual degradation. When he tries to save his daughter from the manager, the manager shoots him, and is acquitted. The estate's (European) doctor pleads with the manager to improve the condition of the coolies but without success. A cholera epidemic leads to further tragedy.

'Chol Mini Assam jabo', an Assamese folk song, also depicts this poignant situation: "Mini let's go to Assam, the land of green plantations. Back home there is too much misery." But soon the family's dream is shattered, and the song curses Jadhuram, the agent, for bringing them to Assam under false pretences.

In the 1960s and 1970s in the Nilgiris, the 'coolies' were better treated and their living conditions were monitored by the state. However, the social and economic conditions were quite different from what they are today. Thimma, who accompanied Ravindran to the firewalking (see page 7) was twelve years old, and his parents had sent him to work in Ravindran's home as a kitchen helper. Compared with the children of other workers, he was seen as privileged.

*Refer to page 6 if you're wondering about the varying fonts.

OUCHTERLONY VALLEY

Extracts from the *Madras District Gazetteers, The Nilgiris,* **Volume I, W Francis (1908) p372-374**

This valley lies in a deep recess under the high western wall of the plateau. It is a well-known and important centre of coffee and tea growing and comprises nearly forty square miles (of which over 7,000 acres are planted up) and contains a population of 5,265 persons. On the east its limit is practically the escarpment of the plateau ; but on the south and north the valley is geographically a continuation of the Malabar district and the Nambalakod amsam respectively, and its boundaries on those sides were at one time bones of much contention. The Tirumulpad of Nilambur claimed that the Nambalakod amsam, the janmam rights in which (he alleged) had been transferred to him by the Nambalakod Valunnavar's family, included the Ouchterlony Valley and also the land on the plateau as far east as the Paikara river. On part of this land near Naduvattam Government were at that period preparing to open their existing cinchona plantations, and for this and other reasons they altogether declined to accept the Tirumulpad's contention. Mr. Herbert Richardson, Deputy Collector of the Wynaad, in 1863 held an enquiry and laid dawn a boundary between Nambalakod, Malabar, the plateau, and the Ouchterlony Valley which came to be known as 'Richardson's line.' Briefly, this started from the Paikara river, went westwards to a rock called Arata Para, thence to the Pandi river, down that to the crest of the ghats, and back to Nilgiri peak. In a suit between Government and the Tirumulpad in the District Court of Calicut in 1868 about the land at Naduvattam (which Government won) this line was an important piece of evidence.

Government were at first disposed to disallow the Tirumulpad's claim to janmam rights in the Ouchterlony Valley, which lay beyond and south-east of this line, respecting, none the less, any titles obtained bona fide from him, in ignorance of the rights of the case, by planters. But eventually, after some years' discussion, they decided in 1878 to abandon all claim to janmabhogam in the Valley, and in 1888 they admitted the Tirumulpad's janmam rights there, Richardson's line being confirmed as the boundary thereof.

The Valley formed part of Malabar up to 1873, when it was transferred to the Nilgiri district. Its revenue settlement was made in 1880 on the principles already followed in the case of the Nilgiri Wynaad.

The Valley is named after Mr. James Ouchterlony, a brother of the Col. John Ouchterlony, R.E., who made the 1847 survey of the district and whose report has often been quoted above. James Ouchterlony was at one time a Judge of the Principal Sadr Amin's Court established at Ootacamund in 1855, and the story goes that the possibilities of the Valley were pointed out to him in 1845 by his brother, who had been greatly struck with a sight of it which he had obtained from the top of the Gudalur Malai at its north-western corner. The whole of it was then an unbroken sheet of forest; and its sheltered position, elevation (from 4,000 to 4,500 feet above the sea on an average), considerable rainfall (80 to 90 inches), rich soil and numerous streams have resulted in its fully realizing the expectations formed of it, the coffee grown there still realizing the best prices of any in the Nilgiris.

The Valley is now such a distinctive and important tract that some account of its history will not be out of place. On the 18th December 1845 James Ouchterlony obtained from the Nilambur Tirumulpad a lease of the eastern half of it (within certain specified boundaries) for the very small sum of Rs. 1,500 down and an annual rental of Rs. 20 ; and the first coffee was planted in what is now the Lauriston estate, in a 'field' which is still as flourishing as ever. A planter from Jamaica named Wright supplied the technical knowledge necessary, and Mr. Ouchterlony also obtained an experienced partner in Mr. A. C. Campbell, who had been a large indigo-planter (and well known pig-sticker) in Bengal and whose family still holds a share in the Guynd estate. He was popularly known as 'Coffee Campbell.' On the 19th January 1857 Mr. Ouchterlony obtained a second lease for another block (also within certain specified boundaries) to the west of the first on payment of an annual janmabhogam of Rs. 2,000. This latter deed however expressly excluded '600 cawnies' of ill-defined land granted to Captain T. H. Godfrey of the Bombay Army, first by two Chettis on payment of Rs. 600, and subsequently by the Tirumulpad (who asserted a superior title to it) on payment of a janmabhogam of Rs. 15.

This grant had already occasioned disputes. Mr. Ouchterlony discovered that Captain Godfrey had trespassed on part of the land included in his first lease, and compelled him to vacate it ; and when he obtained the second lease he entered upon a long course of opposition to, and litigation with, his adversary in the civil, criminal and revenue courts, concerning which amusing stories are told and which was still unfinished at the time of his death, which took place on the last day of the year 1875. A compromise was then effected between his executors and trustees and Captain Godfrey, which was at length embodied in a deed dated 7th July 1877. This recognized Captain Godfrey as the lessee of the 600 cawnies, which had already been parcelled out into eight estates, and also of 3,000 acres in the north-west corner of the Valley, out of which four more properties were afterwards made. The whole of these properties were eventually disposed of to third parties.

Meanwhile the remainder of the Valley had flourished greatly. The preliminary difficulties were immense, for though it is clear that in some remote past the Valley had been inhabited (the stone bull now in the temple near Hope estate and another broken one were found among its jungles, and when the foundations of the bungalow on the Helen estate were being dug, clay images of goats, etc., were disinterred) yet when James Ouchterlony first came to the Valley it was uninhabited. As he himself wrote in 1860–

"There was no resident population within any

accessible distance ; no articles of food to be had near the spot ; we had no roads (properly so called), no police, and no law save at courts too distant to be reached. Labour and food had, in fact, to be imported from a remote district, the first being only obtained with difficulty, and then often scared away by the solitariness of the spot and an undefined dread of evil in the minds of the coolies."

The labour was imported from Mysore, and so was the grain to support it. A depot for the latter was built at Gundlupet in Mysore and a huge store for it was constructed in the Valley itself, whither it was brought painfully by Brinjaris on pack-bullocks along the rough track which was then the only route between Gudalur and Mysore, and which was infested by Kurumba dacoits and wild elephants. Equal difficulty occurred in getting the crop, when it was picked, down to the coast. Elephants and camels had on one occasion to be requisitioned.

Elephants (and other big game) were then very plentiful in the Valley. It is said that Captain Godfrey made much of the money required for opening up his properties from the rewards he obtained for shooting them ; the paths on the Sandy Hills estate are mostly mere improvements of the tracks the animals had made there (elephants, as is well known, have a wonderful eye for the best trace up a hill-side) ; and a cow was once shot from the verandah of the bungalow on the Hope estate, the vernacular name for which property is still Anaikadu, or ' the elephant jungle.' Elephants still come up the valley of the Pandi river to the lower parts of the Ouchterlony Valley in smaller numbers, and in 1892 one was shot by Mr. J. H. Wapshare in the abandoned Montrose estate and one fell into an old elephant-pit near the Umballimalai estate which the Kurumbas had covered over in the hope of catching sambhar. Bison and spotted deer used also to be common, but the opening up of the Seaforth estate in the lower part of the Valley cut off their only path from the Malabar jungles and they are now rarely seen.

Those were the palmy days of planting and the

numerous Europeans (about 20 in all) who were then employed on the estates had (or made) ample leisure for shooting and other relaxations. Once a year they used all to spend a week at the house built by Mr. Ouchterlony at the top of the Valley (known from its materials as 'the tin bungalow') and in sheds built near at hand, where they held a series of gymkhanas. Traces of the race-course are still visible.

After James Ouchterlony's death, however, the property fell on evil days. The trustees for it were his two sons, James William and Gordon Alexander, and the late Mr. H. Wapshare, his son-in-law, who lies buried in the Valley. The two former fell out and went to law (the causes of the dispute are immaterial to the present account) and money which might have been spent on the maintenance and development of the estates went in legal costs. Mr. Wapshare, who was managing trustee, resigned; the High Court appointed an Official Receiver who drew a large salary, had a bungalow built for his special accommodation, but only visited the Valley two or three times a year ; and things went from bad to worse until 1890, when Mr. Wapshare was appointed manager again by the High Court. The two Ouchterlony brothers had died meanwhile. Mr. Wapshare died in 1900 and his son Mr. J. H. Wapshare, who has kindly supplied much of the material for this account of the property, was appointed managing trustee.

Vigorous retrenchments of expenses were then and subsequently made, the European staff being reduced to four and the annual cost of supervision, management and working cut down from about five lakhs to about three. The Ouchterlony Trust is now out of difficulties. Five-sixteenths of it is still in court and the three beneficiaries of the remaining eleven-sixteenths (less certain estates which are held jointly with other proprietors) are Mr. James Ouchterlony's two daughters (Mrs. Johnson and Mrs. Wapshare) and the widow of his son Colonel Edward Ouchterlony, RH.A. The crop in 1905 was as much as 650 tons of coffee and 140,000 lb. of tea, in growing and picking which 2,000 coolies were employed. Ceare, castilloa and para rubber are also being tried in certain estates. The Trust has its own tea factory in the Valley and its own coffee-curing works at Mamalli on the Beypore river near Calicut. Its property comprises over 5,000 acres of opened land in as many as fourteen separate estates, besides a large area not cultivated. The biggest estate is Guynd, an unbroken area of coffee in full bearing measuring over 800 acres. The pulping-house on this, which must be the biggest in South India, was opened by Lord Lytton, when Viceroy, in 1877, as a tablet over the entrance commemorates. Several Governors of Madras have also specially visited the Valley. At Guynd is its post office.

Besides the estates carved out of Captain Godfrey's land and those which belong to the Ouchterlony Trust, there are five (Walwood, Balmadies, Seaforth, Glenvans and Barwood) which were sold by the Trust to others.

Up to 1890 nearly all the coffee was grown in the open ; but in that year shade trees (mainly Grevillea) were planted to check the ravages of the borer ; and most of the Valley now looks, from above, as like an unbroken forest as it did before any of it was opened up. Shady paths and roads innumerable cross and re-cross in every direction under the trees, streams and rivers pour down from the plateau to the east (in several cases over beautiful falls) and the place is one of the most picturesque areas in the district. A bridle-path runs down to it from Naduvattam past ' the tin bungalow ' and a District Board cart road enters it from Gudalur, crossing the Pandi river by a girder bridge erected in 1899 at a cost of Rs. 17,000.

QUEEN BEA

She lives in a time-warp, alone with her dogs in the heat and humidity of Southern India, but things are not what they were

Words and Pictures CAROLYN SLOAN

I should have met Beatrice Wapshare 25 years ago: we were both planters' wives in the Ouchterloney Valley in South India, a remote area below the Western wall of the Nilgiris hills. I even saw her once as I drove back from Ooty three hours distant. British planters were thin on the ground then, and I was amazed to see another European woman in the Valley.

"Ted and Bea Wapshare? Forget about them!" I was told, "they're recluses." The Wapshare family were legendary; they'd once owned the whole valley and more. But the Empire had crumbled and its survivors were strug-

Beautiful Bea in modelling days (above), married Ted Wapshare (right) "to get rid of him". Now she rules The Valley alone

AN ARTICLE BY CAROLYN SLOAN HOLLIS IN *SAGA* MAGAZINE IN 1993,
FOLLOWING A VISIT TO INDIA TWENTY-FIVE YEARS AFTER SHE LEFT.

I should have met Beatrice Wapshare twenty-five years ago: we were both planters' wives in the Ochterlony Valley in South India, a remote area below the Western wall of the Nilgiri hills. I even saw her once as I drove back from Ooty three hours distant. British planters were thin on the ground then, and I was amazed to see another European woman in the Valley.

"Ted and Bea Wapshare? Forget about them!" I was told, "they're recluses." The Wapshare family were legendary: they'd once owned the whole valley and more.

But the Empire had crumbled and its survivors were struggling to live in a genteel manner in the ruins.

Ted's mildly eccentric sisters, Dot and Queenie, ran an Ooty mansion as an hotel which tended to fall down several rooms at a time. Vague, pale-eyed brother Bob had a tea estate, and I sometimes met him on the ghat road hitching a lift from somewhere to nowhere.

Bea and Ted were still hermits when we left India but as time passed I heard Ted had died suddenly of gastro-enteritis and Bea was out and about socially, playing tennis in her seventies and running an estate alone. Now seventy-nine, she has a strong claim to be the only British planter left in India. Returning to India after twenty-five years, Bea was high on my list of 'important relics' to visit. A quaint, charming, very English lady who has not been home for thirty years. She dresses elegantly, thanks to relatives who buy clothes for her from M&S and send them out to her. Over gin slices she gossiped mischievously, chided me for not calling on her twenty-five years ago, and invited me to spend a day on Compton, her tea estate just off the Ooty-Mysore road …

"I'm an old fashioned lady in an old fashioned house with an old fashioned garden," was her greeting. All true. Her bungalow is daintily wallpapered, homely memoirs share space with Wapshare heirlooms and rosewood furniture made in the Valley in the old days. Her cottage garden is neatly picket-fenced. She lives alone, apart from her servants – and a lot of dogs … "How many, Bea?"

She hesitated and counted, "Fourteen, with the guard dogs!"

She is justifiably proud of the estate, 50 acres of lush, high quality tea undulating over the hills. Striding the paths, waving a stick, her tough planting character shows a spirit she has needed in life that sounds just like a plot for a romantic novel …

In 1950, a pretty RAF widow, and a former Max Factor model, she was running a smart Kensington restaurant when Edward Wapshare came to lunch. An erratic romance followed. "He came every day after that and became a nuisance," she told me. The twinkle in her eyes echoed in her voice, "I think I married him to get rid of him!"

She had no idea how strange and hostile his family would be. His ancestors had gone out to India in the 1840s when Col. John Ochterlony, R.E., surveying below the Nilgiris, discovered a sheet of virgin forest with its own river and streams. At a perfect elevation, about 4,500 feet with 80 inches of rain a year, it was ideal for the burgeoning tea and coffee industry. His pioneering brother, James, planted it up, importing labour and food from distant Mysore. His daughter married an assistant planter, Henry Wapshare, and at the height of their prosperity the family owned twenty-one tea and coffee estates, thousands of acres of jungle, and valuable land and property outside the Valley including a palace in Ooty.

In the late 1920s, tea prices slumped, disease plagued the coffee and the presiding Wapshares were ill-advised and ill-equipped to manage. Virtually anyone who wasn't a Wapshare faced a slow downfall that is still discussed today. "They thought as long as they had land they'd survive," a young planter told me, "they could go and spend, spend in UK! They sold estates to pay debts … lost them in poker games with maharajahs." Bea thinks there is some truth in most rumours, and they certainly and mysteriously 'gifted' their palace to the Maharajah of Mysore. "It's a hotel now. Go there, you can see the plaque," says Bea.

Ted's father died of a broken heart when he lost The Valley, leaving his widow and children ailing properties. Ted got Burnside, the last valley estate. When Bea arrived in 1953 she was horrified at the dilapidated state of her new home. She said, "All the fine things I brought out ended in the auction room!" Ted had gone to India six months ahead to warn his family he had married. "He was the only one who dared. The others had their romances, (some scandalous, as Bea likes to relate) but they were stopped immediately

BEATRICE WAPSHARE AT WORK ON HER ESTATE.
ORIGINAL PHOTOGRAPH BY CAROLYN HOLLIS. COMPTON ESTATE 1993

the family knew about them. They didn't want anyone to come into their property." Bea soon got the message.

"I'm a lady. I'm an Ochterlony-Wapshare," Queenie liked to proclaim. "But who's Bea? Just a girl Ted picked up in London!" Other British planters openly ostracised her but Bea was a survivor then, as she is the sole survivor now. "I braved the storm and rose above it. And everybody tells me now that if it hadn't been for me there'd have been no Wapshare property left today. I've kept the Wapshare name alive, and I've done it with dignity.

Sophisticated, London Bea loved planting life and wanted to get involved. "Ted wouldn't hear of it. "You don't need to know anything," he said, "we don't teach women to be planters!" Ted wouldn't even teach her Tamil, though he spoke seven Indian languages himself.

"I used to walk around with him; I had no idea I was absorbing knowledge but I was," she recalls. When Ted had a heart attack Bea was on her own for four months. A tea field needed pruning, so she consulted his records and had it pruned. "When Edward came back he was stunned. 'Who told you to do it? You've done it all wrong!' he said. I nearly fell through the floor! I thought I'd done a good job and I had really but he wouldn't admit it. When he died in 1972 I knew exactly what I had to do."

The family didn't intend Bea to inherit Burnside. "They'd have packed me up like a parcel and sent me home." But she and Ted had foreseen problems and circumvented them. With a small sum of insurance money she set about increasing the coffee and improving the tea, driving the green leaf to the factory herself in an old Standard Vanguard.

"Nobody knows how I worked. When people say, 'Aren't you lucky to have all this,' they don't know, you know."

REMEMBERING

Carolyn Hollis continues

Meanwhile, I had dreamed of going back to the Ochterlony Valley. In the 1960s my husband managed the most distant tea estate in the Valley, beyond stretched unexplored jungle. There was just one small estate beyond it, whose owner kept changing the boundaries and encroaching on Seaforth land, and tribal people.

Some planters' wives found it lonely and the towering hulks of the Nilgiris oppressive – they said they moved closer at night. In my memory it was hauntingly beautiful. An ex-planter phoned me, "Don't go back to the Valley, I beg of you!" he pleaded, "You'll come back with tears in the eyes."

But I had been in India for six weeks, seeing how much – and how little – had changed. The major tea company's estates were impressive, with computerised factories, high-tech hospitals, even television in some bazaars.

The Valley road is so broken that what was a forty-minute journey now takes one and a half hours. Landmarks, wild sholas and ancient 'protected' trees, had gone. The estate my husband had left prosperous and profitable in 1968 is still independently owned but long ceased to be a sterling company. Cash is very short and it shows in the tea, factory, schools, bridges, hospital, but above all in the labour. Fewer people are working and twenty-five years of progress have by-passed their standards of living. As ever in rural India, the curious stare at foreigners. But then, I thought, the last English woman they'd seen was probably me.

The present manager battles gamely; but his bungalow is falling apart and big carpets I remembered jig-sawed by white ants. Seven servants have been reduced to one and he turned out to be my grinning old kitchen coolie brought out of retirement.

Water is short. Apparently the waterfalls our children tried to count as they cascaded from the hills during the monsoon no longer fall. Even the panoramic views are obscured by the government's ubiquitous eucalyptus planting scheme. Yet there is something timeless and indestructible here. Its time will come again one day. I didn't leave with "tears in the eyes," but I could understand how Old Man Wapshare died of a broken heart when he lost the Valley.

A LOFTY OCCUPATION

"Empty!" muttered John Partridge superciliously, spitting out a mouthful of tea liquor on to the wheel-mounted spittoon. Selvamani, our head teamaker, looked down resignedly at the floor, even as he continued making notes, while the Englishman moved on, firmly declaring his expert opinion as he sipped one cup and then the next.

I was back in Prospect, back at Woodbrook. Partridge, was manufacturing consultant of Forbes Ewart and Figgis, Tea Brokers. As a consultant, his duties were to assist factory managements in tea manufacturing and also appraise them of what the market needed from time to time in terms of grades, sizes or liquor qualities as required by his employers. He was engaged in assessing the cup-quality of Prospect tea, which at the time was being exported exclusively to the UK. Selvamani had been recently flown in from Ceylon with the mandate of bringing flavour up to par. That morning, preparing for this important visit, he had laid out twenty-five sparkling-white handle-less tasting cups in a straight line on the long wooden table. Into each cup, he carefully spooned 2.5 grams of tea, weighed in a jeweller's balance, from the sample tray. He then poured fresh boiling water to the brim of each cup, covering it with a lid. To cover the last cup would have taken five minutes from covering the first one, and the first cup would now be ready for its infusion to be decanted into a tasting cup. Once the tasting cups were all filled, Selvamani would empty the infused leaf from the brewing cup to the upturned lids, spreading it evenly and wringing out any liquid by tightly pressing with a wooden disc. These would now be placed in a line above the brewing cups.

On small wooden trays in front of each cup were samples indicating the grade of tea awaiting approval for dispatch to the company's brokers in Cochin, where they would be sold to the highest bidder in auctions conducted by brokers, and exported to the UK.

Public auctions have always been the primary method by which tea plantations sell their unblended bulk produce to a range of buyers in a competitive manner. The taster's assessment is generally found to be an accurate reflection of the value of the product and the price it will earn at the auctions, and is therefore highly valued. When Partridge declared that the first cup was "empty", it meant that the tea liquor had no substance. It lacked fullness. Clearly, the tea had been withered for more than twenty hours in warm weather, or it had been insufficiently rolled. Selvamani had a few more choice, if hurtful, words thrown at him that day, drawn from the glossary of tea-tasting terms approved by the Tocklai Research Station, in Jorhat, Assam. Another cup was dismissed as being "tired" – the tea had become flat and unfit, having passed the stage at which it would have been classified with optimal maturity. Such observations spell trouble for the batch of teas already manufactured.

Tasting tea is a technique that requires great skill; it is practised by few and perfected by even fewer tea-trade professionals who taste extensively as part of their job. An

BOB SAVUR ASSESSES THE FLAVOUR
OF HIS TEA AS PART OF HIS DUTIES
AS MANAGER OF KODANAD ESTATE IN
1985. FROM SAAZ'S ALBUM.

astute sense of smell, highly discerning taste, and sharp eye for detail, all accentuated by experience, helps the taster decide the quality of each of the hundreds of samples he or she will taste through the day, day after day.

The process of tasting tea is quite amusing to watch. It begins with a quick reading of the appearance of first the dry leaf and then the infused leaf. The taster then sniffs the empty brewing cup, assessing its aroma, before moving on to the tasting cup. Drawing a sip of tea decoction into the mouth with a loud slurping sound, the taster rolls it around, retains it for a short time, and then spits it out. The purpose of the noisy slurp is to ensure that the tea hits the upper palate where its worth can be simultaneously evaluated by both relevant senses: smell and taste. Tea tasting is highly subjective but, like any skill, it is acquired through long years of practice, and the tasting of innumerable cups each day in the course of the job. It is said that, to be a good taster, one must refrain from smoking, drinking alcohol, eating spicy food, and any other activity that would corrupt one's senses of smell and taste. As manufacturers of tea, it was important for estate managers in charge of the factory to be adept at tasting so that they could understand the observations of the taster and send accurate communications regarding every batch of tea dispatched to the brokers.

The old Ooty haunts

The first time I spent a day at the Ooty races was with my colleague and bungalow-mate, Firdous Darashah. Ooty was a small tourist backwater, but during the racing season it became quite glamorous and urban because the racing crowd, many of whom had holiday homes there, would come to stay and lend their sophistication to the sleepy hill station.

The Ooty race course had been built by the British in 1886. Spread over 50 acres, it served as a summer pastime for the Raj when the Madras Presidency functioned from Ooty. Most popular at the paddocks were the thoroughbreds and Arab stallions, with their rippling muscles, from the Kunigal stud farm owned by the Maharaja of Mysore. With many of his subjects working on the tea estates, the Maharaja was a significant if unseen presence in the Nilgiris. Over the years, he had bestowed large tracts of the land he owned in the area as gifts to loyal subjects. Chamraj Estate and Royal Valley Estate near Gudalur were two of such properties. In fact, it was through his connection to Mysore that Firdous, formerly a manager of the Ideal Jawa factory, had taken up a position in the tea plantations, but he soon returned to the world of horseracing where his heart lay. Vijay Lad, another senior colleague at Prospect, was also from a family with racing connections – his father, Major Lad, was a horse trainer par excellence with the Maharaja of Gwalior. In 1972, Vijay quit the planter's life to join the Royal Western

India Turf Club in Poona as a racing official.

With Ooty just 20 miles away, Nana, Cyrus and I would drive there every Sunday, alternating between Nana's Fiat 100 Millicent, Cyrus's Ford Consul and my beloved two-door Standard Herald for the journey each week.

My father had bought me the Herald in 1971, and drove it from Madras to Bangalore and on to Mysore, and up the ghats to Naduvattam, along with my brother Unni. He was sixty at the time – in those days considered to be quite an advanced age – and it was a feat. The company had, with effect from 1 July 1969, very graciously increased the recoverable advance to purchase a motor car as well as the monthly allowance, so I was able to take advantage of the perk with my flashy two-tone painted car, bright red above door level and brilliant white below. The car stood out in Ooty and it was difficult to get away with mischief! While it also had a fantastic engine, there was an inherent flaw in its suspension as was the case with many cars of the time and the stub axle would give way quite often. The spider joint also gave me endless trouble. A breakdown meant waiting by the side of the road for help in all kinds of hill weather, but, back then, people would always stop and offer a hand, even if it meant pushing a car in pouring rain until it started. I drove the car on 9 June 1973 to High Forest Estate in the Anamallais on transfer, and sold it in October 1975, just before I got married. Before that, there were many trips we made in it from Prospect to Ooty!

In Ooty, we always had lunch at Shinkow's Chinese restaurant, the poshest place in town in those days, followed by a movie at Assembly Rooms, the only cinema in the Nilgiris which screened English films. Tickets for seats in one of the two private boxes (Assembly Rooms still offers these relics of a bygone era) were sold from the exclusive 'Box Office' window and not the usual counter which invariably had a queue in front of it. After the movie, we would walk down Commercial Road, dropping in at Radio Corner. Raju, the owner, stood at the door looking smart in his trademark polo-neck shirt and belted trousers, and always had a special smile for his favourite customers, young dorais from Prospect, who had come shopping for the latest music which in those days could only be had on long-playing discs (LPs) or the smaller 45 RPM records. There was an Irani restaurant next door, where we'd enjoy thick, strong, milky tea with samosas, occasionally dropping in at the nearby department store, Chellarams, to pick up odds and ends. No trip to Ooty would be complete without visiting the crowded Ooty market and buying the best cuts of beef – undercut or sirloin – to take home and enjoy on Monday and Tuesday since, in an era where a refrigerator was described as "a Scientific Marvel" (as in the image overleaf), they would not last much longer into the week.

Occasionally, we would stop by at our regular haircutting salon, a place we called Bulganin's. The person who cut our hair was N Varadhan and, though in India's despicable caste hierarchy (which was still quite prevalent at the time), he might have been dismissed as a lowly barber, our Varadhan was a charming and well-spoken person to whom a large population of the Nilgiris, and in particular most of us planters, turned to for the essential periodical requirement of a haircut. A visit to Bulganin's almost always turned out to be a social event because there would be others waiting their turn there, sitting and leafing

It's a
Scientific
Marvel

No matter where you live, you can have all the modern benefits of Refrigeration with ELECTROLUX. This dependable refrigerator can be operated by kerosene, electricity or gas.
Available in four sizes: 1⅓, 3, 5 and 7.5 cu. ft.

Electrolux

HARRISONS & CROSFIELD LTD.
(INCORPORATED IN ENGLAND. LIABILITY OF MEMBERS LIMITED)
Quilon, Cochin, Kozhikode.

FROM *PLANTING DIRECTORY OF SOUTHERN INDIA*, UPASI, COONOOR (1956)

through magazines provided by Varadhan, and he would introduce us with gentlemanly courtesy. A large photo prominently displayed on the wall showed Varadhan shaking hands with Nikolai Bulganin, Prime Minister of the erstwhile Soviet Union, the USSR. It had been taken in 1955, when Bulganin had toured various parts of India along with Nikita Khrushchev, then Communist Party Secretary. It was a historically significant visit, being the first time that Soviet leaders made an official visit to a developing country that was not socialist. The memories it created have lived on in many small pockets of India, and here, at our salon, we often made Varadhan repeat the story of how he was taken in a car to the Governor's summer bungalow in Ooty, Raj Bhavan, where the Soviet leaders were being hosted for two days, and gave Bulganin the haircut of his life.

Another Ooty haunt was the Gymkhana Club, where we would stop for beer and a game of billiards. It was a great place to meet with planter friends, and we sometimes met people holidaying in Ooty from the plains and would invite them home for a meal to give them an experience of life on the estates. This club has a 200-acre golf course, very popular on the golf circuit but very difficult to play due to its undulating and often steep terrain on the gently rolling downs that surround Ooty.

Since 1845, these downs, situated at a height of 7200 feet above mean sea level, have been used for the primeval sport of fox hunting. Beagles and fox hounds were trained to take part in the ceremonial hunt for which riders wore red jackets and, since Ooty had no foxes, would set out to hunt down a jackal. The Ooty Hunt was a great social event and exists in a reduced form even today.

My years on Woodbrook were a time revelling in the glory of nature as I took the first steps to establish myself in my career and formed special bonds with my colleagues. One of these was Nana Menon, an exuberant, fun-loving person who later went to live in USA and recently moved to Colombia. Before Nana, my bungalow-mate was Victor Dey who joined Prospect in December 1967. He was also a brilliant and fun-loving young man, from Madras like me, and we got along very well.

Victor recently reminded me that back then Woodbrook was also known as Doraisani Thottam – the Mistress's Garden. And this reminded me of a time when the management decided to plant a new field in Belle Vue, a division of Liddellsdale, with a vegetatively propagated clone, C-1 (Chamaraj-1). As the undergrowth was cleared for the planting, I noticed Dasa maistry pausing with reverence at a large doddamaram stump and taking extra care to clean and polish its unusually smooth surface. He explained to me that this was where a doraisani of olden times would sit to take a break from her relentless and all-weather supervision of planting activities, sipping coffee she poured out from the flask she carried with her. Ever since its rediscovery, the stump was referred to as 'doraisani kuttu katte' – the mistress's tree stump. Perhaps it was the same British lady who had once lived in Woodbrook; perhaps it was she owned who or managed Belle Vue.

One time, Victor and I were travelling to Mysore on my Jawa. The road leads through a large game reserve with an interstate line running through it, placing Mudumalai in Tamil Nadu and Bandipur in Karnataka. These national parks were established in the 1940s and formed a vibrant ecosystem replete with many wild animals including elephants, tiger, Indian gaur (which we generally referred to as bison), leopards and a variety of deer. That day, in the middle of Mudumalai forest, the chain of the bike came loose and slipped off. Victor, driver-cum-mechanic, took out the toolkit and began fixing it. As I waited on the side of the road, I noticed an elephant approaching. Sensing danger, Victor and I suddenly became as strong as tigers and between us ripped off the entire chain guard and threw it aside, scooting off before the advancing animal could catch up with us. We were later told by forest guards that the elephant, a lone tusker, had been

VICTOR AND RAVINDRAN WITH
THEIR BIKES AT WOODBROOK.
IMAGES COURTESY VICTOR & JINI DEY

84

seen playing with the chain guard as a child would with a new toy. By then, of course, we were safely back in the haven of Woodbrook.

Sadly, today the quaint old bungalow is just a shell of what it once was, and even the chimney stack that once emitted smoke, signalling to all around that it was a home and not just a house, can no longer perform the function it was built for. The kitchen garden that once fed us with its bountiful crop of strawberries lies barren today, and the Amaryllis, Arum lilies and Agapanthus that once lined the brook of Woodbrook are all gone. What has lasted is the friendship that Victor and I continue to share. And some years ago, another Amaryllis bloomed in nearby Wynaad – a resort run by Victor and his wife Jini, an earthly paradise where they live and host holiday seekers from around the world who come in search of peace and tranquillity.

Ref: No. 1/2A.

The Estates & Agency Company, Ltd.

(Incorporated in England — Liability of Members Limited)

TELEPHONE: OOTY: NADUVATAM-24
TELEGRAMS:
 MANAGER, PROSPECT, NADUVATAM.
POST & TELEGRAPH OFFICE:
 NADUVATAM (4 MILES)
RAILWAY STATION: OOTACAMUND.
LONDON REGISTERED OFFICE:
 LEE HOUSE, LONDON E. C. 2.
AGENTS & ATTORNEYS IN INDIA:
MESSRS MATHESON, BOSANQUET & CO., LTD.
 COONOOR-1, NILGIRIS.

PROSPECT ESTATE & P. O.
NADUVATAM
(NILGIRIS, S. INDIA.)

2nd February, 1968.

Messrs. K.S. Medappa, Vijay Lad and M. Ravindran.
Prospect Estate.

Dear Sirs,

Motor Cycle Accidents.

I append below an extract of a recent letter received by me from Agents:

"The Board are very disquieted with the number of serious motor cycle accidents that have taken place in the Company during the last year or so. Whilst appreciating that there will inevitably be minor accidents on estate paths in the normal course of supervision, they would however like to make it quite clear that in future serious accidents due to carelessness and/or excessive speed will be treated as avoidable injury and the Assistant concerned may be held responsible for the cost of repairs to the machine and under certain circumstances even forfeit his salary for the period he is absent from his duties. In an earlier circular we have already advised you with regard to the use of crash helmets and the liability for medical expenses that may arise if this instructions is ignored. We are pleased to note however that generally the value of crash helmets is appreciated. "

"A fatal accident would be a tragedy. Treated with reasonable respect a motor cycle is a most useful form of transport for supervisory purposes."

Yours faithfully,

Manager.

LETTER REPRIMANDING THE PROSPECT BIKERS, FROM THEIR NEW
MANAGER, BOB SAVUR, DATED 2 FEB 1968.

A JAPANESE PROJECT AT PROSPECT

In 1971, E&A decided to build a green tea factory on Liddellsdale in collaboration with a Japanese company.

THE JAPANESE GREEN TEA TEAM AT DINNER WITH BOB AND SITU
SAVUR AT THE WEST DOWNS BUNGALOW. SITU, WHO HAD JUST
RECENTLY PERFECTED SIR JOHN'S DEMANDING MENUS, NOW
LEARNT TO PREPARE LARGE QUANTITIES OF RICE AND SUITABLE
ACCOMPANIMENTS FOR THESE HONOURED GUESTS. SHE WOULD SPEAK
ABOUT HOW THEY MUST HAVE EXPERIENCED INDIAN HOSPITALITY
IN THE PAST BECAUSE THEY WERE TERRIFIED OF BEING ASKED IF
THEY WOULD LIKE SOME MORE. ONE OF THE JAPANESE ENGINEERS,
WHEN HE WAS APPROACHED BY THE BUTLER FOR A SECOND HELPING,
WOULD PICK UP HIS PLATE AND RUN AROUND THE TABLE.
THIS IS A COLOUR PHOTO, RARE FOR THE TIME, PROBABLY TAKEN WITH A POLAROID
CAMERA AND PRESENTED BY THE JAPANESE TEA EXPERTS. FROM SAAZ'S ALBUM.

A godown – warehouse – on Prospect was cleared, and machinery temporarily erected to produce samples of green tea for assessment by the Japanese representatives. A suitable site was identified close to TR Bazaar and LS Kumar and Nana, respectively manager and assistant manager of Liddellsdale Estate, were responsible for setting up the factory, right from excavating the land, constructing the building, laying out the machines and

INAUGURATION OF THE PROSPECT GREEN TEA FACTORY BY SITU SAVUR ASSISTED BY VIJAY LAD. FROM SAAZ'S ALBUM.

commissioning them, with technology and supervision from Date Iron Works of Japan. A Japanese engineer, Isamu Amikura, and a technician, Kenji Shibata, arrived to install the machinery, which was imported from Japan. They were accommodated at the snooty Ooty Club, and were chauffeured back and forth in a company-owned brand-new white Ambassador car. Towards the end of 1972, we E&A managers, dressed in our best suits, arrived for the grand inauguration of the Green Tea Factory. Entering the factory, we were surprised to see Mr Date, the owner of the Japanese company, lying under a faulty dryer to repair the problem in the electric heating coils that had arisen due to the fluctuating power supply. He extended a greasy hand to greet us but remained where he was, focussed on the task at hand right through the speeches and applause of our opening ceremony.

When the fully automated factory started functioning, there was a lot of enthusiasm from the Japanese. Somewhere down the line they lost interest in the project and the venue eventually shifted to Prospect where Moroccan/Chinese-type green tea were produced for other markets around the tea-drinking world using conventional machinery with a few additions, though with less automation.

The green tea factory soon became a relic. Its ruins still adorn the main road from Gudalur to Ooty.

Terramia Estate. "Young Tea."

Terramia Estate. "Pruning Tea."

TERREMIA ESTATE AND FACTORY IMAGES FROM *ILLUSTRATED GUIDE TO THE NILGIRIS*, HIGGINBOTHAM & CO, MADRAS (1905)

FOR ANYONE WHO LIKES AN OUT-DOOR LIFE

Excerpted from *Illustrated Guide to the Nilgiris*, **Higginbotham & Co, Madras (1905) p113**

For anyone who likes an out-door life, a planter's lot on these Hills can barely be beaten (when everything goes well with his crops). His day usually starts at 7 or 7.30 with "Roll Call" of the coolies, sending them out in proper gangs for the various works. He then goes around the various fields to see that his orders are being properly carried out, and usually remains out till 12 and then on a Tea Estate goes to the Factory to weigh the morning's leaf. After seeing this, and the leaf properly spread on the racks, he goes back to his Bungalow for breakfast, after a short rest goes out again to see that the weeding, etc., measured and that the tasks have been properly done, then to the Factory or Store to weigh the leaf, or in the Coffee season, the cherry.

Terramia Tea Factory and Coffee Pulping House.

T. Stanes & Co., Ltd.

Post Box No 12.

Telegrams: "STANES".　　　　Telephone Nos. 22 & 372

COIMBATORE

Branches at :—Cochin, Coonoor and Kotagiri

'A' Class Pool Agents of the Coffee Board
Estate Suppliers and Shippers

Dealers in :

Agricultural Fertilisers, Cattle and Poultry Foods,
Asbestos Cement Products, Hessian,
'Nilgiri' Brand Portland Cement, Jute Twine,
'I.C.I.' Plant Protection Products, Leaf Bags and
Coir Matting, Hair Belting, Rubber Belting and
Leather Belting, V. Belts and Hose,
'Phynazol' (Substitute for Phenyle), Tarpaulins,
Spraying Materials, Estate Tools, Tea Chests,
Bulking Sheets, etc.

TEA QUOTAS AND INSURANCE

Fertiliser Factories at Tudiyalur and Vypeen.
Storage Facilities for Cochin Tea Auctions.

FROM *PLANTING DIRECTORY OF SOUTHERN INDIA*, UPASI, COONOOR (1956)

If he has not had time during the day to attend to office work he now attends to this, and then back to his Bungalow to enjoy a well-earned rest.

Sport, as a rule, enters in greatly to a planter's life, and if he takes out a licence (vide Game Laws) he can enjoy both small and big game shooting. In the interests of Sport, the planter has allowed the depredations by Game to cost him a pretty penny, and the Sambhur perhaps is the worst offender ; invariably delighting in the destruction of Shade Trees, which now are necessary for the cultivation of Coffee and the planter has yet to discover a suitable shade which the Sambhur will not mutilate!!!

Messrs. T. Stanes & Co., of Coimbatore and Coonoor, are the wholesale and retail agents for Terramia Teas which have gained three Gold and one Silver Medals for excellence, a postcard either to this Firm, or to the Manager, Terramia Estate, will receive prompt attention.

A VERY SPECIAL VISITOR

My acquaintance with leeches resumed at High Forest. And with elephants, too – after all, we were in the Anamallais, which means 'elephant hills' in Tamil. What I had not expected at all was an exquisite miniature deer that somehow wandered into the drawing room of my High Forest Estate bungalow one evening. What a surprise – and what a very special visitation! It seemed churlish to stand up, even to offer a glass of rum as one might to a special visitor; instead I sat right where I was, trying not to move and disturb it.

The delicate creature stepped in on its pointy toes and, sensing no danger, moved towards the dying embers of the fireplace, sniffing articles in the room as it went.

The colonial-style bungalow at High Forest, built like the others in the tea districts of South India by the British, was as old as the tea there – nearly a hundred years old. The bungalow designs were said to be replicas of the ones built in Ceylon where the British had established tea plantations a few years before they started planting in the Nilgiris. The tile-roofed bungalow had open verandas all around it and gleaming red floors that were constantly polished with Cardinal wax polish. Tucked away in the midst of Mudis properties and bordering Kerala, High Forest received over 3000 mm annual rainfall – the highest in the area. Accordingly, every room in the bungalow had a fireplace where wood was burnt not only to keep the residents warm but also to prevent damage to the soft furnishings and other parts of the building from fungal attack. All executives were issued a monthly issue of fire wood. Acacia decurrens, a type of wattle, was most preferred as it burned even when freshly cut and green while other varieties such as the wood of grevillea (silver oak), eucalyptus, and the conifers needed to be dried well before they would burn. I still remember the fine fragrance which came from the aromatic oleoresins, and the sudden loud crackle of cypress when the resin in it popped in the fire.

Leaving my visitor by the fire, I stepped out as quietly as I could. It had occurred to me that the poor animal must have entered this unfamiliar habitat in search of food. I took some vegetables out of the 'meatsafe' – a wooden cupboard with doors of mesh that allowed air to circulate and kept food fresh, and left them by the door.

FROM *PLANTING DIRECTORY OF SOUTHERN INDIA*, UPASI, COONOOR (1956)

When I woke next morning, I was alone in the house again. The vegetables had been nibbled at, and the beautiful creature had left, but only after depositing a few droppings on the carpet, perhaps as a way of expressing gratitude.

Chevrotain or mouse-deer, the smallest hoofed mammal in the world, stands at about two feet off the ground and weighs from 1 kg to a maximum of 8 kgs. They are unique animals and today are nearly extinct – but a sighting was rare even fifty years ago.

Lacking in agility due to their thin short legs, they are said to forage meekly and tentatively under plantation canopy, feeding exclusively on plant material. In an area teeming with predators like foxes, jackals and panthers, the chevrotain lives in harmony with nature, learning to fend for itself from a very young age, even to the extent of dropping in on a rainy evening for potluck at a planter's home.

HEAD-HUNTERS, INDIGO PONDS, AND A MIRACLE

Not long after the historic mouse-deer visit in 1973, I was sitting in my field office when a Muthuvan tribal walked in wearing nothing but a white mud-splattered mundu. He had a large bottle-gourd shell slung across his back and the severed head of a Great Indian Hornbill hanging alongside. He offered me both for Rs20, opening the gourd to show me that it was full of pure forest honey. Thinking it over, I offered him Rs10 for just the honey. He rolled up the note I gave him and slid it into a bamboo pipe hitched to his waistband (an unreliable wallet; tribals have lost entire savings of paper money to termites when stored in similar contraptions). He then handed over the gourd and walked to the nearby shop to spend what he had earned, the hornbill head – as fresh and brightly coloured as if it was still alive – swinging behind him as he went.

Much of the land claimed by the British for the tea plantations was once jungle, so thick that light could not fully penetrate it, and home to all manner of animals. Some of the people to whom these areas are an ancestral homeland have been designated as scheduled tribals, and continue with their semi-nomadic lifestyle even to the present day. The Muthuvans have lived in these high ranges for centuries and are as familiar with every contour of the hillside as an urban child would be with the route between home and school. Equally native to this region is the Great Indian Hornbill. These large and strikingly beautiful birds nest at heights and command the valleys as they swoop in flight from one hillside to another. At High Forest and, in later years on the other estates in the area where I lived and worked, sightings of these majestic birds were common as they glided overhead like celestial couriers. With a wingspan of five feet and a weight of nearly four kilograms, their wings flapped as noisily as a steam engine, and could be heard from as far off as 100 metres. With their impressive size and colour, their regal beak and crest, they are a natural choice for ritual worship. I wondered how the Muthuvans

FROM *PLANTING DIRECTORY OF SOUTHERN INDIA*, UPASI, COONOOR (1956)

lay their traps for the birds, and what precise ceremonies might have been conducted by the person who visited me that morning. Was there a divine reason that this particular bird had not achieved its potential lifespan of fifty years? The British had introduced hunting as a sport in these hills – and it was the British who later designated some areas where shikar – hunting as a sport –

Original photograph of a hornbill by
Neeta Kiran

was permitted, and other areas as reserves where animals lived under protection. The Great Indian Hornbill would somehow survive to one day become the state bird of Kerala. These were matters too complex to pass judgement on this typical day in High Forest with the sun shining bright and rain persisting in dripping down at intervals.

The hill tribes lived in clusters of hutments in a valley. They were separated from us by a huge gorge through which the perennial Idamalayar River flowed – not just separated but in fact isolated from us, because the only way across to the other side would be a tree trunk – perhaps one that had fallen across the river, or one held in place with stones and pegs of wood, packed together tightly with mud. This swinging bridge was easily traversed by the tribals – though never attempted by anyone else!

The river formed the boundary between Tamil Nadu and Kerala, where implementation of strict forest laws prevented entry into the area which had been declared a sanctuary, and it thus remains one of the best-preserved rainforests of India.

The gushing river was just as challenging to a swimmer as the tree bridge. However, there were bright blue pools formed by huge bowls of rock, and in summer when it grew hotter than we were accustomed to in the hills, they beckoned invitingly. We would climb carefully down the slope, my friend Dharmaraj (who worked on the neighbouring estate) and I, sometimes joined by visitors. We would leave our clothes at the water's edge, and slip ever so slowly into the freezing cold water which had left the mountain but retained the temperature of Anaimudi peak's 8800-foot altitude. In the crystal-clear blue-green pond, shoals of colourful fish swam peacefully around us with an occasional nudge or caress.

In the 1970s, life in High Forest was tranquil and followed a simple routine coloured by occasional dramatic acts of nature. One day, in the course of a fierce thunderstorm, a massive bolt of lightning struck a tall tree on the top of the hill. A large branch, splintered by the bolt, flew up into the air and came straight down, lodging itself in the fork of the tree and forming a huge cross that was visible for miles around. People poured in from long distances to view this miracle.

It was the British who had brought Christianity to India. Some of the best schools in the country were built by the missionaries, alongside their churches. While providing various facilities such as help with sustenance and life counselling, they welcomed families and communities into Christianity. In Injipara, several years later, I remember evicting Michael, who had usurped an estate shed in the Upper Division to house his cows. The shed had been built to shelter about twenty cows of the workers in that division with a provision for one cow each, and its calf for as long as the calf was feeding from the mother. Michael was the only one using the shed for his three cows. At the same time, a need for a church had been voiced by some of the workers. On the basis of disciplinary action under the Industrial Disputes Act, Michael was evicted and the shed was converted into an All Saints' Church (somewhat reminiscent of the manger of Bethlehem). At the inauguration, I was presented a lovely silver bowl, a memento which continues to adorn my drawing room.

Buses were now bringing in pilgrims, and sightseers too, to view the spectacular cross that nature had wrought on the mount. Locals quickly took the opportunity to set up tea and snack stalls. The conical loudspeakers of the day began to blare out instructions and announcements in between film and devotional music. Bewildered wild boars, jackals and bison stumbled out of their tranquil abodes and caused the crowds to leap in fear and excitement. It was a taste of the times to come, an era that lay thirty years in the future. At the time, the steep slope proved too much of a challenge for the revellers who wanted to go and touch the cross. Gradually interest waned, nature weathered the miraculous cross back to its elements, and our lives continued as before.

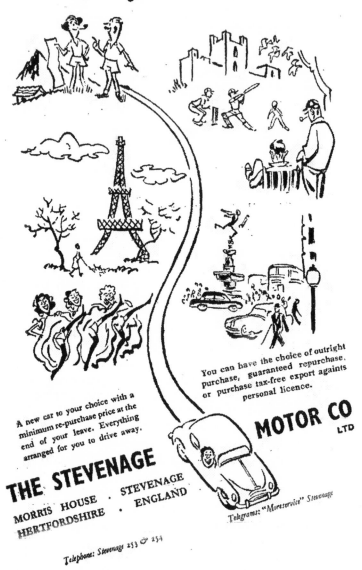

REPRODUCED FROM *PLANTING DIRECTORY OF SOUTHERN INDIA*, COMPILED BY
THE SECRETARY, UPASI, COONOOR (1956)

A VISIT FROM EDWARD LEAR

Excerpted from *Edward Lear's Indian Journal, Watercolours and extracts from the diary of Edward Lear (1873-1875)* Jarrolds, London, 1953 p194-196. Edward Lear is best known for his nonsense verse but his diaries make interesting reading, too!

SEPTEMBER 30 1874

Slept pretty well, considering one kept all one's clothes on. Washed, got tickets and tea, and luggage weighed and labelled. Off at 5.30; flat plain, palmyra palms by the million. Mile 250; mountain ranges afar, some isolated, some in long lines. Plain becoming much more beautiful, the long chain of western ghats stretching all across the view onward. What queer groups of carved horses round holy trees. Nilghiris beyond, and showing far more varied forms, it seems to me, than any part of the Himalayas. 332nd mile; Metapallayam. Pretty scenery; very thick jungle, cactus, acacia, etc.; mountains above, all wooded. Reach foot of Coonoor Pass and find two tonjons waiting, six men to each and two extra. Cry of bearers: a hay home, a ho home, a he home, a high home, a hay home. This vast gorge is a wonder for fullness and beauty of verdure. Several coffee plantations alongside the road, the first I ever saw; like dwarf laurels. I think it was 5 when we reached Davidson's Hotel at Coonoor, where a croquet ground with many Albanas and Albani were somewhat alarming. Walked about a good deal with Mr. Davidson; the scenery is very close, serene, and grand in many ways, though nothing here is equal to what I saw in the lower part of the gorge, the rocks and vegetation there being quite glorious. There was a Colonel Baker at dinner who had been six years at Trichinopoly and had never seen the temples, and a coffee or tea-planting cove who talked principally of dogs.

OCTOBER 1

All Coonoor seems totally undrawable as Indian scenery; it is not unlike Bournemouth here and there, but with different foliage. A deep ravine stretches below Davidson's Hotel; various houses are scattered here and there, roses and other flowers abounding. Trees also for a time but gradually becoming nil. When the road reached Tiger Hill above the opening of the gorge, or great valley, the view over the southern and eastern plains is magnificent, perhaps somewhat resembling that from Mussooree. I made two small sketches.

OCTOBER 2

Waited, and got angry, for tea. Drew at the end point of Tiger Hill. After tiffin read papers till past four, the weather being overcast and cloudy, and growing more and more so. It was too late to draw again at Tiger Hill, so I thought to get a drawing of the church only, but just as I reached the place I wanted to stop at, down came torrents of rain. I and Giorgio stood up below a tree, which for a time sheltered, but eventually wetted us more than might have been the case had we walked back. As the sun set, I walked up and down the beautiful garden walks, dark as it was; yet, from the colour of masses of poinciana and other flowers, still a gorgeous gloom. Unbeknown animals, frogs, beetles or birds, making very strange noises, which Giorgio aptly compares to the clicking of an anchor when weighed. Dinner singularly pleasant; conversation on Greek and other subjects. So may pleasant people compensate more or less for various hotel nuisances.

OCTOBER 3

Off in two tonjons, or high chairs: coolies undulating; much discomfort at first. Lovely forest and plain view, but did not stop, hoping to draw it on my return. Mountains suddenly clouded, and rain ahead; provoking. Began to walk back, but could do nothing but qua sketch except the very merest scribble. Heat great; ghat very steep. Lunch; but rain came on suddenly and spoiled salt and bread, and what was worse, in moving to shelter I kicked down the claret bottle and lost half. Frightfully slippery much and great toil.

OCTOBER 4

Agreed, as it was clear, to walk to Lady Canning's seat; a point of the hills so called. A lovely walk through jungle woods, where tree ferns and other matters were delightful, but there was a world of mist, and hardly anything visible; nevertheless, from what little one could see, the view must evidently be truly wonderful and some of the foliage is quite exquisite. Giorgio has a cough, which distresses me. Dinner very pleasant, at first at least, the conversation was only irrigational and agricultural. Captain Winterbotham, a sensible practical man, lent me the last Home News. In it is the death of Sir Henry Storks, and when I remember his never failing kindness to me from 1861 to 1864, I - even in this India - am sad. Strange life, ours.

OCTOBER 5

Reached Ootacamund and the Alexandra Hotel. Giorgio, of course, goes out without his hat, and gets fresh cold. Ootacamund is prettier than I had expected, but is just like an English place, such as Leatherhead. Got a very good breakfast, beefsteak and claret; afterwards, slept a wink, and then wrote letters. A curious place is "Ooty"; houses stuck all about the hills, and trees everywhere, which is not what I was led to expect. At the library a vast many carriages are waiting, and Albanas were driving everywhere with the usual full dress and double syce accompaniment. Then I went to the church, which is very picturesquely situated; and next to a photographers, where I got two photographs. After all this, half deaf of cold, I walk back. "Ooty" is far more varied and perhaps more picturesque than Coonoor, but is so English as to be, I think, utterly undrawable.

OCTOBER 6

Went out with Giorgio, moony-moony, and down to the bazaars where there are really fine vegetables. What to do here? Some view of the church, and some other general view; some martyrdom at the Governor's, inevitable, necessary, proper. The morning is perfectly lovely, and doubtless, where families or individuals can live quietly here in good villas, I can quite understand the immense blessing such life must be, after the hot and unquiet existence at Madras or on the plains. After breakfast, we walked around but only saw three very dirty, blanketed females with long glossy hair and very ugly faces. By this time it was 1, and they sent a peon to show me the way to Lord Hobart's. I resisted a carriage, for the roads at Ooty are odious, full of unsuspected pebbles, that jolt and martyrize individuals with such physical conditions as this child has. Got up to Government House, after a very long pull, and sent in my card; shortly received very kindly, but all were at tiffin. Lord Hobart I remember at Lord Strangford's, quiet and simply good:

TODAS ARE AMONG THE ORIGINAL INHABITANTS OF THE NILGIRIS.
ORIGINAL TODA PHOTOGRAPHS BY KANCHANA SUNDERARAJAN,
OOTY 9TH MILE 2014

Lady Hobart much nicer than I had been led to expect from Delhi acquaintances. After tiffin, drawing room, and talk; walked down to Alexandra Hotel and found there a note asking me to lunch at Government House from Lady Hobart! So, I had to write to say I had never got it until now, and my appearance at luncheon and in the middle of it was purely accidental.

Rainbow Trout at Konalar

The little-visited Grass Hills of the Anamallais are swept with winds of such high velocity that trees do not grow there. Tribals occasionally visit to harvest grass, which they use to thatch roofs and make baskets. The adventurous trek from Eravikulam in Munnar to the Konalar fishing hut in the Grass Hills was forbidden by the state government even forty-five years ago. However, four plantation friends and I did it in 1975 with special permission from JC Gouldsberry. John, a decorated hero of the Second World War, was the founding spirit behind the creation and preservation of the Eravikulam National Park. A classic conservationist, he was committed to protecting the ecosystem, the lifestyle of the tribals in the area, and responsible shikar. As a senior manager of Vaghuvarrai Estate of the Kannan Devan Hills Plantations Company, Munnar, he was also one of the last remaining Englishmen to have stayed on.

Twenty years later, we grabbed the opportunity to do the trek again, this time in a larger group including two of us who had done it before, and our daughters, and this time walking in the opposite direction. It was a chilly morning, early in the year, and we carried sandwiches, snacks and water for the two-day trek, staying overnight in the Konalar fishing hut.

The trek skirts around Anaimudi, the tallest peak in South India. Eluding access to most climbers due to its topographic isolation, and nestled amidst a number of wildlife sanctuaries and forest reserves, the spectacular monolith surprises the trekker by suddenly baring its massive crown around a curve on the narrow path.

It is impossible to describe the beauty of those endless mountains with their ravines, rivulets and gorges. We walked on elephant paths most of the time, but sometimes found ourselves creeping along narrow ledges with a sheer drop at dizzying heights. And there were stretches when we waded through grass so tall that we had to virtually tunnel our way through it.

These treks were highlights of the many visits we made to Konalar and the Grass Hills which were a favourite picnic spot for planters in the region. We would drive to the hut in a very basic Willys four-wheel-drive jeep, originally devised for the requirement of a vehicle that

A GROUP OF TEA ESTATES INDIA EMPLOYEES ON THE WAY THROUGH THE GRASS HILLS TO KONALAR.

could traverse almost any terrain, by the United States military. It leapt and bounced across the seemingly endless grasslands – in many places the grass grew higher than the jeep – clung on to slippery rocks and splashed through shallow rivulets. We followed the snaky mud tracks laid by others before us, which transform into rivulets during the severe monsoons of the area. On one visit in the 1990s, the jeep overloaded with revellers, we arrived at Konalar late in the evening. There we slept on a bare cement floor, unprepared for the temperature dropping to what felt like less than 0°C, and fighting all through the uncomfortable night for a share of the threadbare blanket we found in the hut.

We had come to Konalar to fish for the rainbow trout it was famous for. Rainbow trout, a species of salmonid and native to cold-water tributaries feeding the Pacific

DHARMARAJ, RAVINDRAN, DR BENJIMIN, HIS SON THOMAS, THEIR
MUNDU–CLAD MUTHUVAN GUIDE, GRASS HILLS 1975

Ocean in Asia and North America, was introduced by the British planters into some of the high-altitude rivers of India. Its tender flesh has a delicate nut-like flavour. Hours of perseverance failed to yield the smallest fry or fingerling, no matter how many times we changed the bait, line, or sinker! As lunchtime approached, morale sank lower and lower. Eventually it was my friend Anil Dharmapalan (arguably the least-skilled angler amongst us!) who saved the day. He summoned Perumal, the watchman of the hut – and, incidentally, the sole human presence in Konalar – and took him aside. Picking up a netted bag of the type used for plucking tea leaves from the floor of the jeep and a bottle of rum from our stocks in the hut, he whispered something into Perumal's ear

The Konalar hut. Note the bottle gourd full of honey in front of the group.

109

ABOVE: THE TEI EMPLOYEES AT THE FORD BUILT BY PERUMAL, 1995.
BELOW: CAROLYN HOLLIS AT THE SAME POINT ON THE STREAM,
THIRTY YEARS BEFORE.

and handed them to him. Perumal shot off into the dark and in next to no time reappeared with a bag full of slithering trout, their pink flesh visible through their skin.

While the men rejoiced in the blazing bonfire, the ladies in the group (for this is the way things were done in my time) sautéed the fish over it in butter, lemon and parsley, concluding the recipe with a flourish: flambéing the dish with the famous 'Perumal' brand rum.

At some point during the revelry, the secret was disclosed. Perumal, who lived an ascetic existence all the year round, looked forward to the occasional visits from well-heeled fishermen like ourselves. As the merry jeep-load approached, bouncing along the off-road track, Perumal would quietly prepare the scene by fording the river upstream. And then, when the moment was ripe, all he had to do was lean over and undo his handiwork, helping himself to the bounty of fish that had accumulated there and hand it over to his hungry guests.

KEEP
CALM
AND
DRINK
TEA

An enormous lake in our backyard

When India gained Independence, one of the many efforts of the new government was to build infrastructure. The first prime minister, Jawaharlal Nehru, an old-world statesman and orator known for his way with words, coined the phrase 'Temples of Modern India' to describe dams and hydro-electric projects, steel plants and scientific research institutes, in his speech at the inauguration of the construction of the Bhakra Nangal Dam. It took three more decades to bring this vision of progress to the plantations and it so happened that I was living in the area when a dam was built across the Suruliar River in 1977, and experienced in full what happens before, during and after the building

Original photographs of Suruliar by Dr Arulnathan

of a dam. This particular dam created a large reservoir across Highwavys, Manalaar and Venniar estates, resulting in breath-taking scenes of tea, water and jungle that supported a huge population of wild animals, with elephants, bison and sambar being the most frequently spotted. The thousands of people who lived in the area were affected in different ways. Plans to construct the dam included the decree that all homes that lay within the Full Reservoir Level (FRL) must be evacuated well before the construction began. Bulldozers and earth excavating machines worked at full speed, roads were re-laid and tarred, and bridges were built. And I, as manager of Manalaar Estate, where all the buildings and labour lines had originally been built near the river, was responsible for relocating hundreds of people who had been living in this settlement for generations. Dozens of homes, the crèche, school, dispensary, cattle sheds, co-operative stores, muster shed, estate office, labour recreation club, group staff club, central stores, and group workshop had to be reconstructed. At the same time, new land had been made available during the process of building the dam

and these fields were being planted by newly-recruited labour who also needed to be housed. While temporary sheds were hastily erected, they had to be quickly replaced with standard units that conformed with the requirement of the Plantation Labour Act, which specified that each family be allocated a minimum space of 348 square feet and a toilet using waterborne sanitation. We also located new sources for water supply, built new storage tanks and made arrangements to supply protected piped water to the structures being constructed. Every unit was also provided with electricity.

All this was a huge task and we managers worked hard, moving from our plantation role to the role of building construction managers, which we accomplished with the help of semi-educated but skilled and versatile contractors including Joseph P Nunez, Papa Boyan, Karuppu Boyan, Palani Boyan, Virumandy Thevar and others. Timber was sawn from our own jungles by about twenty sawyers under contractor Thankappan. One unforgettable character was Mr Arputhaswamy, flamboyant proprietor of the transport agency, fondly referred to as 'brother'. Hailing from the idyllic village of Royappanpatti, Arputhaswamy supplied us with loads of cement, iron, sand, tiles and bricks from the plains. His lorries also supplied petrol, diesel and coal to the factories, and took back loads of tea for sale to the various auction centres. Arputhaswamy was a proud alumnus of St Joseph's College, Trichy, and he was as colourful as he was erudite with the Tamil epic Thirukkural, from which he quoted liberally. We feasted together on biriyani with chicken fry followed by kulfi-falooda at Taj Hotel, Madurai, and enjoyed his conversation. Arputhaswamy was an exponent of Nadi Joytisha, a type of astrology practiced in the region, in which the astrologer reads out predictions from old texts with clairvoyant skills. One of his predictions, that crude oil would flow from the gulf under the Arabian sea into India in the near future, is still remembered with amusement by managers engaged in the major construction activity of those days.

During that time, I was witness to a freak accident which resulted in tragedy. A large tree was sawn down and it keeled over with a mass of it roots being torn out of the soil as it fell. A sawyer climbed into the hollow cavity from which the roots had emerged, to chop off the taproot and separate the trunk from its connection to the ground. The man trimmed peripheral roots as he made his way to chop the taproot, when with no warning and at lightning speed, the tree sprang back in place and the man was trapped inside the bowl. Dozens of co-workers sprang forward to tunnel into the cavity and to chop down the trunk as fast as they could, but by the time the sawyer was extricated, it was too late. The case was naturally investigated by the police, and treated as a death in harness, with the company paying compensation to the bereaved family as per the applicable rules.

The dam gave a new geography to the area, and the estate workers, who had lived a ten-minute walk away from the field, now had to walk fifty minutes around the reservoir. The main diet in the past had comprised greens and vegetables, but now there was plenty of fish available. New occupations arose as people took to fishing and selling fish. Some sporting fellows built canoes and coracles which they monetized for leisure and for transport. Water was now readily available: we could pump it out of the reservoir and fill tanks, using chlorine to make it potable. The water table had risen, so the wells dug lower down the hill would continue to provide water even in the dry season. At dawn and dusk, animals came to the water's edge to enjoy the rays of mild sun and drink their fill before retiring to the jungle. Otters and other aquatic animals came to stay, and the population of snakes increased. And so it was that the changes in topography altered lives completely, not all of it in a bad way.

ORIGINAL PHOTOGRAPHS BY DR ARULNATHAN

THE LADY DOCTOR AND THE BABY ELEPHANT

On 4 March 1970, an ex-army officer, Captain Ranjini Kumar, took up the post of Lady Medical Officer at the Highwavys Hospital and moved into the bungalow allocated to her on the estate. Doctors are an integral part of the estate infrastructure and take care of the resident labour, and every well-run estate employs a qualified and experienced doctor for this essential function. A 'lady doctor', as they were called in those days, was a particular asset. Indian mores made it inappropriate for male doctors to attend women in labour and babies were born at home under the care of a traditional midwife, generally a woman who had facilitated the birth of hundreds of babies and was highly skilled. Still, mortality was high, hygiene standards were questionable, and Tea

Estates India introduced a rule that childbirth must take place in a hospital with scheduled antenatal and postnatal check-ups, and systematic training on important aspects such as hygiene and anaemia. In such circumstances, a 'lady doctor' was a necessity.

After the customary welcome dinner at the Group Chief Medical Officer's bungalow, Dr Ranjini and her husband, Colonel Kumar, retired to their new home. But early next morning, they were woken by a telephone call from the hospital, informing them that they must on no condition step out of the house.

In those days, a telephone was a luxury commodity. In the cities of India, a five to seven year wait for a telephone line (or even longer) was expected, and involved an application and repeated follow-ups. A connection was so hard to get that fathers reportedly gave them as part of their daughters' dowries. Telephone lines had been laid in the Highwavys in the 1950s and 1960s, and the factory, the hospital, the senior managers and the estate doctor had been issued connections with wall-mounted cranking phones with fixed mouth pieces and detached ear phones. Centralised exchanges in the factories were maintained by the factory electrician. In the 1970s, these were replaced by

ORIGINAL PHOTOGRAPH BY DR ARULNATHAN

government telephones and local fifty-line capacity exchanges. (Historic two-digit and three-digit telephone numbers are recorded in documents on pages 24, 40, 86, 92, 100 and 257 of this book.)

Receiving a phone call was generally quite a significant affair! Dr Ranjini was now informed that she could not leave her house because there were elephants outside. This was when she and her husband realised that the loud elephant sounds they had heard the previous night were not a regular occurrence in this elephant homeland, as they had assumed, but an elephant in labour!

It later became clear that there were a group of female elephants camped in Dr Ranjini's kitchen garden. One was a new mother and the others had assisted as midwives, and were now serving as a security and support team. Perhaps they had previously conducted a reconnaissance trip, and identified the uninhabited bungalow, with plenty of vegetables and a water source in its kitchen garden, as an ideal location for a temporary maternity ward. The elephants stayed on for three full days, conducting the mysterious activities of postnatal elephant husbandry, and left perhaps after the little one could walk unsupported. During that time, the hapless couple, who may have experienced army sieges in the past, found themselves trapped inside. A worker from the factory, who was reputedly adept in such matters, would stealthily deliver a tiffin-carrier packed with food for them from one of the other manager's bungalows.

What a wonderfully auspicious welcome for Dr Ranjini, one that the labour force took as a sign that she had brought with her good luck and prosperity for them!

POUNDS OR KILOS? METRES OR FEET?

Many of us continued to use units of measurement inherited from the British. One of the questions on the written test for a position on Prospect asked:

> Sugar is bought at Rs 125 per quintal and sold at Rs 1/35 per kg. What percentage of profit is made?

India had converted to the Metric System in stages with acts passed in parliament as early as 1958. Nine years later, the arithmetic question on the test paper was perfectly legitimate. Even today, many of us understand altitude more comfortably in feet than in metres.

In March 1976, when I took over as assistant manager of Upper Manalaar division, the charge of building labour quarters fell on me. Until then all measurements were in the British foot-pound-second (FPS) system. Now, hundreds of houses were going to be constructed, and the company decided that all measurements would be made using the metric system. This involved measuring freshly sawn timber – one tractor load each day – for payment to the contractor; measuring the finished woodwork such as doors, windows, roofing and other for payment to carpenters; both cubic and flat measurements of masonry work to pay the contractor, and more. Road tarring, painting, and even the spacing of plants now had to be done using metric measurements. There were endless calculations to be made and the changeover was tedious and often frustrating. However, the discipline was essential and its successful implementation prepared us to easily integrate when we faced computerisation two decades later.

MAINOTTAM: AN ART FOR THE SUPERIOR SLEUTH

Under the Plantation Labour Act, it was mandatory for the management to issue a bar of soap to workmen of designated categories such as pesticide sprayers, sweepers and others to wash their uniforms and personal clothing.

Chinnappan, the sweeper who was engaged to sweep labour lines on High Forest, had more ingenious ways of using the soap issued to him. Pluckers would come home for lunch at about 12 noon, open the locks on the front door, enter leaving the key in its keyhole, and rush back to work after a hurried lunch and having locked the house before they left.

This gave Chinnappan plenty of time to slide by, pulling out a key from the door he had selected for the day, and making an impression of it in his handy cake of soap. He could then have a duplicate key made at leisure. And during working hours, when the lines lay deserted, he could enter the house and steal money and other valuables. Several such thefts left the police clueless and frustrated, until they engaged a Mainottam specialist.

Mainottam is an ancient technique which incorporates hypnosis and séance. The practitioner puts questions to the subject, who sees images and answers, narrating a sequence of events, as if in a dream. The word mai refers to kajal – collyrium – or ink, and nottam means to look. Mainottam involves coating the smooth side of a betel leaf with fine black soot by holding it above an oil lamp. Oil is then smeared on the soot, to make it glisten, after which a young boy or girl is called upon to peer into the reflective surface and observe the images that start to emerge. Quite often the child recognizes people and narrates live movements of a missing person or recreates crime scenes just as if they were being live-streamed on the leaf.

Within a few minutes of starting the Mainottam, Chinnappan was seen on the small black betel leaf screen, waiting for the pluckers to go into their houses. He was then seen pressing the keys into his cake of soap. The police quickly apprehended him, and his confession sealed his guilt.

Just a few months later, in Upper Manalaar division, it was Chellapandy Thevar who cracked the case of theft of four spraying machines by employing Mainottam. A spraying worker who had been dismissed was found to be the culprit. Chellapandy, our night watchman, was a small-time magician with a bushy moustache that spread over his cheeks, concealing a natural hole in one of them. He was a Mainottam specialist with several successes behind him and rose to be respected as a great seer until alcohol got the better of him, after which his reputation suffered greatly.

A NEW PHASE IN THE LIFE OF THE ERECTION ENGINEER

Rajam and I got married on 22 October 1975. Earlier that year, High Forest had been taken over by Mahavir Plantations, which was owned by a north Indian family of Kochi who were in the tea and spice trade. In those days, the Anamallais had a large number of estates bordering on each other, and planters had options. I wanted my new bride to be a corporate wife rather than the wife of a planter at the beck and call of a proprietor from a traditional Indian business community who might not encourage modern methods of management, and was able to find a good position in Tea Estates India, a company which owned a number of tea estates and had Brooke Bond as their agents in the UK. Two weeks after our marriage, I joined Davershola Estate as Assistant Manager and, in April the following year, was transferred to Manalaar Estate, named for the river that flowed through it.

Situated high on the leeside of the Western Ghats between Munnar, Thekkady and Kodaikanal, the Meghamalai hill range stands at a height of 5000 to 6000 feet above mean sea level. The British came to Meghamalai – the cloud mountain – in 1920, and began planting tea. They named the range Highwavys, and in time it became home to some of the finest tea plantations in the world, sharing its name with one of them. With the nearest town being 50 kilometres away and a lone tortuous road leading to the place, however, it had few outsiders.

It was March 1976 when Rajam and I drove in our 1970 beige (second-hand) Ambassador from Gudalur to Highwavys, which in those days was in Madurai District. Our bungalow in Upper Manalaar division was situated halfway down a huge slope of tea that looked like a lush green carpet. From the cypress hedge bordering the large lawn, we could see the verdant expanse of the dense jungle across the hill, and the Suruliar river running right below. The house was a beautiful colonial structure, but it had no electricity. The company provided a generator which worked only from 6 to 10 pm and we were unable to use our toaster or record player. We had been provided a refrigerator that ran on kerosene but it was so old that the Freon gas had stopped circulating. Ashok Broome, a planter on a nearby estate, advised us to place the machine upside down as he had found it worked that way – but somehow we never got around to trying that out.

How did Rajam, a Bangalore girl, adapt to this wilderness in an ancient, rambling home which did not even have a refrigerator? How did someone who was used to calm and temperate weather all year round cope when faced with the fury of nature?

On a day less than two years after we were married, we drove to Madurai with our six-month-old baby Arjun. Torrential rains were common in our area but that day, 18 November 1977, howling winds and lashing rain shook the hills to their foundations. We could see some parts of the road had slipped down into the valley, and in others earth had fallen on to the road from the hillside, restricting roads to dangerously narrow widths. The journey took much longer than usual.

Driving home through pelting rain and whistling winds late that night, along with a colleague and his wife, Thomas and Shirani Jacob, was a nightmare. Dense mist coupled with dim headlights minimised visibility, making the climb through the tortuous roads perilous. Just short of centre camp, a half-way point with a water source where vehicles and people could take a break, there was a huge landslide blocking the road completely, and I was forced to bring the car to an abrupt halt. Jolted out of deep slumber, Shirani remarked with amusement that she had never seen a landslide so close before. Hardly had the words left her mouth when a deafening noise akin to thunder broke out from above, of land mass snapping away and stones falling above the car. In seconds, another massive landslide fell just behind the car, bringing with it rocks, trees and large volumes of soaking wet soil.

We spent that night sleeping in the car, stranded at a height of 5000 feet, sandwiched between two landslides. Winds bellowed eerily around us, rains hammered down, and many more landslides fell in the vicinity. We could see water flowing down the rock by the side of the car, blocked from flowing further down the hill by the fallen earth, and we could see it rise menacingly around us. Sporadic lightning lit up the skies through the night like strobes.

We would later learn that our night of terror was a mere shadow of the destruction that had taken place on Diviseema, a sleepy island on the eastern coast of the Indian peninsula near Koduru in Andhra Pradesh, where the shoreline suddenly takes a curve inland as if to let the mighty Krishna river into the Bay of Bengal. Its location and proximity to the bay makes it particularly vulnerable to persistent tropical storms and cyclones during which unrelenting torrential rains and battering winds lash the island with punishing severity. On that night of 18 November, the deluge and storm left a trail of annihilation. At the peak of its intensity, the wind speed exceeded 200 kmph, and a storm surge of 18 feet of sea water flooded over Diviseema, resulting in the death of nearly 15,000 people. More than a hundred villages were completely destroyed, leaving a staggering 3.5 million people homeless. Thirteen sailing vessels including some foreign ones went missing along with their crew members. We were nearly 900 kilometres away from the epicentre of that terrible storm and had experienced one of its outlying tremors. We were rescued next morning by Varkey, the main contractor of the Suruliar hydroelectric project, who happened to be passing by in his jeep. To our further good fortune, Arjun had slept through it all like an angel, unmindful of the entire nightmare.

It would not be a complete recounting of the story unless I mentioned that it was not only the occupants of the car who were saved that day but also the trunk full of cash in the boot, six lakhs withdrawn earlier that day from Indian Overseas Bank, Madurai, meant for Diwali payment to the employees of the Highwavys Group!

CLUB LIFE

One of the most redeeming features of living in an isolated place was the vibrant social life we enjoyed at the Highwavys Club. Still, even that had inherent risks! One new moon night, Rajam and I were returning home from a club night and our car had a flat tyre at a granite quarry on the way.

In the hills, the night skies, unobscured by artificial light or urban landscapes, are a celestial palanquin rich with the mysteries of astronomy, the enchantment of mythology, and the aesthetic wonder of brilliantly glittering constellations! The plantation bungalows, mainly situated on hillocks, provide a wide vista of the surroundings and the entire horizon. By November, winds drive away the mist, fog and rain-bearing clouds, setting the scene for cold days in which land and air become bone dry. The sky becomes azure, clear, deep blue, and often quite cloudless. Sunsets are spectacular and every colour of the rainbow is seen in the clouds. And at night, the brilliant moon and shining stars emerge. The Milky Way reveals itself, night after night, in celestial splendour! In later years, when our children came home for their holidays, we enjoyed learning names and stargazing together. Our son Arjun would be the family astronomer, often teaching the rest of us about galaxies and lesser-known stars.

That night, however, the stars shone intermittently behind the clouds. It was completely still and silent. And there was only one way to get home – by walking. We began climbing an uphill slope to the bungalow two kilometres away. As we turned a corner, the smell of elephant dung assailed us and we soon saw the road splattered with it. Was it a herd or a rogue on a rampage? Either way, our lives could be in danger. We stepped carefully, surrounded by shadowy shapes. After an excruciating journey of several minutes, we approached the muster shed and could hear the night watchman, Chellapandy Thevar, singing loudly to himself. We began to giggle in relief at the thought that any elephant out there would have run away rather than listen to this! Escorting us to the bungalow with his foot-long Eveready torch lighting the path ahead, he told us that a large herd had just walked past.

Rajam and I began our married life in a place with elephants crossing our path and many parties to enjoy. But life on a tea estate was invariably very lonely. Even when there was more than one bungalow on an estate, none was close enough to walk across to borrow a cup of sugar. The Nilgiris, with estates spread even further apart, had been lonelier. I remember the first 'tennis meet' we had on Prospect, arranged by Bob Savur, LS Kumar and Ramaswamy, the latter from a family of tennis champions. Even Ramoo's mother was a formidable player, unimpeded by her sari as she leapt up or stretched out to smash her opponent's serve! Tennis meets were a tradition in the Meppadi, Mango Range, O Valley and Gudalur Clubs, instituted by British planters as a club affair. Participants would bring sandwiches, potluck and snacks for the day while the game went on. Later the ladies of Mango Range took the lead in hosting a proper lunch. In 1969, planters from Seaforth and other estates drove up to Prospect and the matches were held at tennis courts in West Downs and Liddellsdale. The day was spent playing tennis and enjoying the feast prepared by Anandan, Bob's butler, under his wife Situ's supervision! As the sun rose in the sky, however, crows began to hover, cawing and creating a racket that threatened to dominate the day. Just then, Ram Adige drove up in his Standard Herald. Parking and stepping out, he assessed the situation. Then, without saying a word and true to Ram's style, he opened the boot of his car – or 'dicky' as we called it in those days! – took out his airgun, aimed carefully and down came a crow with a noisy flapping of feathers as it fell. The reverberations of the shot died down, the remaining crows flew away, and the tennis continued uninterrupted.

B NATARAJAN AND KS MEDAPPA REPRESENT NILGIRI-WYNAAD AGAINST NILGIRI TEAM KEN BALOO AND VIJAY LAD AT THE WELLINGTON GYMKHANA CLUB TENNIS COURT, UPASI, 1969. MEDU IS SEEN IN THE UPASI SPORTS CLUB COLOURS. HE HAD JUST RETURNED FROM A HOCKEY MATCH AGAINST THE STAFF COLLEGE TEAM.
IMAGE COURTESY SUNANDA LAD

Life at Prospect was quite isolated but for us at Manalaar, the Highwavys Club was a noisy refuge which we thoroughly enjoyed. Built for the executives of Tea Estates India and their families, the club was small but immaculate, and formed an oasis – a literal watering hole – in the midst of our lush green tea plantations. It was beautifully maintained, right from the polished brass knob of its front door, which led into a burgundy-carpeted foyer with a wood-burning fireplace blazing a welcome to visitors. A glistening tambour clock sat on the mantelpiece and there was a well-stocked bar in the corner. The adjoining door opened up to a table tennis room, the walls of which were lined with glass-fronted bookshelves. The stuffed head and pelt of a large saddleback ibex hung on the rear wall.

Sporting activities were the life of the plantation clubs. A planter who excelled at sports would always be

RAJAM, NANDITA, ARJUN, RAVINDRAN, HIGHWAVYS, 1981

more respected than his peers. Tennis, golf, billiards and
badminton were extremely popular until, as the 1990s
proceeded, cricket became a national craze and, perhaps
fostered by television, replaced them all. Planters' clubs
were places where style and fashion were important,
and men and women both dressed up to attend social
events. On special occasions, we would all bring specially
cooked dishes from home and make an evening of it. We
would drink, dance and socialise, and followed traditions
inherited from the departed British, such as celebrations at
Christmas and New Year's Eve. We even had an egg hunt
at Easter! And it took a nationalist like NC Kankani, the
general manager at Sholayar Estate of the Birla-owned
Jayashree Plantations, to be the first to host an annual
Diwali party with the traditional fireworks, sweets and
other festivities.

I remember the preparations we made for the 1981
Christmas Eve party. Our son, Arjun, was four, and
our daughter, Nandita, a baby just one year old. A
black dachshund, Gurang, completed our family. Our
neighbour GP Reddy, Group Manager of the Highwavys
Group, owned a dalmatian named Bozo. We were good
friends and our dogs got along well too.

Peter, a clerk in the office also lived nearby and he had
purchased a duck which he had been fattening up for his
family's Christmas lunch. Seeing the hectic preparations
the masters were making, the dogs conferred and devised
a plan of their own. While our rollicking Christmas Eve
party unfolded at the club, Gurang and Bozo, not to be
outdone, got together and stole Peter's duck, took it to
the boss's bungalow, and had the party of their lives too.
Peter woke to an empty cage. Shocked and distraught,

he accused Reddy's gardener Ammavasi, of having stolen his duck. Ammavasi denied the charge and quietly went about his work with an injured air. He was vindicated soon enough when he came across the remnants of the poor duck in the bungalow garden. Exhausted after their wild binge the previous night, the two dogs dozed through the day and woke in the evening with huge hangovers!

MANICKAM

Manickam came to work as a ball boy at the Highwavys Club when he was just eight or nine years old, in the 1920s. He began by picking tennis balls – a job more difficult than playing the game itself – and went on to marking the tennis lines as a 'marker'. 'Manickawm,' as

MANICKAM IN CIVVIES, WITH PLANTERS CMR DANIEL AND
RAVINDRAN ON EITHER SIDE, HIGHWAVYS CLUB, 1995.

the expatriate planters pronounced his name, soon learnt
to play, and made a skilled practice opponent who, due
to our social conditioning, would never be considered
suitable to participate in a club match. Almost without
anyone noticing, Manickam began helping out at the bar
and, as his skills grew, he took over the coveted post of
barman. As a young bartender with an unlimited stock
of imported spirits at his disposal, it was but natural that
the 'club boy' should develop a taste for cocktails; he also
developed a reputation for integrity that matched his
skill at pouring exact shots without measuring them.

Manickam was already in his eighties by the time my
family and I were frequenting the club. He continued
to respond to the call 'Boy!' as he had always done, and
his childlike enthusiasm and endless energy did indeed
justify the title. He remembered the good old days with
fondness – but his commitment to his present job never
wavered. On club nights, Manickam would open the
door to guests, fully liveried and with shiny brass buttons,
a warm smile complementing his perfect 'Namaskar'. It
was he who kept the club running and made sure its

ORIGINAL PHOTOGRAPH OF HIGHWAVYS CLUB BY DR ARULNATHAN

red floors were always gleaming with red cardinal polish. In the billiards room every baize was brushed, the balls spotless, the cues well-chalked and the score board shining, to welcome the billiard buffs on club evenings. A master cueist himself, the 'club boy' would leave his opponents standing in a challenge even after he had had a few sundowners!

When the evening was well warmed up, Manickam would rustle up a 'club supper', an early version of the all-day breakfast, from the small club kitchen. Maggi noodles, eggs of your choice on buttered toast, baked beans, sausages, and sautéed tomatoes – each dish available at a price of Rs4.50! And, when the evening (which would invariably spill into the early hours of morning) was done, it would be Manickam who would on occasion warn you that elephants had been sighted in the vicinity. And he would wish you a warm "Good night!" as cheerful as his welcome had been when you entered in the evening.

Manickam was in his nineties when he died, still the 'club boy', much beloved of a wide span of generations of Highwavys Club members.

KEEP
CALM
AND
DRINK
TEA

Collateral damage

In 1983, when we moved from Manalaar to the neighbouring Venniar Estate, Gurang naturally came along with us. Being new to the estate, he established his territorial rights by sniffing at workers passing by, barking at people whom he

ARJUN, RAVINDRAN'S SON, WITH THEIR PET DOG GURANG

found needed chiding, and chasing stray cows, dogs and strangers whom he wished to keep away. This done, he only had to lie at the bungalow gate while the workers who filed past on their way to work in the mornings acknowledged his reign by maintaining a respectable distance.

Venniar, too, was close to the jungle and elephants roamed freely. One evening, Gurang did not return home after his customary evening stroll around the labour lines and visits to his various friends. Search parties were sent out in various directions and came back with the tragic news that Gurang had been found dead. It appeared that he had taken shelter under a concrete skirting drain in a vacant staff quarters to allow a herd of elephants right of way. Sadly, despite these precautions, he had been trampled upon and was killed. It was a tragedy for our family and left a deep void until much later, when Gurang-II, an exact replica, came to us.

We did have another close encounter with an elephant, nowhere near as tragic, but which left its mark. It was a year when our children were still young and I decided that it would be a brilliant idea to arrive as Santa Claus for the children's Christmas party riding on the back of an elephant. What a thrill it would be for them!

There were tame elephants working in a nearby timber camp, so we sent for an elephant from there, and it duly arrived, accompanied by its mahout and a helper, at the group manager's bungalow where I was waiting with my friends. One of the prerequisites of Santa-hood is that one must be sufficiently inebriated to remain in high spirits through the ordeal of being strapped with pillows and helped into the costume, cap and beard. In fact, it is a documented tradition among the planters of South India that a bottle of rum is mandatory on such occasions and if it can possibly be emptied before the proceedings begin, so much the better. Dressed as Santa, clutching onto a sack full of gifts, I proceeded to the location near the club where the elephant was waiting. The mahout got the elephant to kneel, and I was pushed up to a position from where I could clamber on to its back and pull myself up into sitting position. One of them put a rope into my hands and, winding the other end of it around the elephant's neck, motioned me to sit astride the elephant so that he could then tuck my feet too into the rope. He then patted the elephant on its back and it slowly lumbered up. I felt the earth moving beneath me. It was a strange wobbly feeling as, with all four legs of the elephant in motion, everything under me seemed to be shaking! And – why had nobody ever told me before how sharp the bristles on an elephant's back were? I was being jiggled up and down, dodging the sharp tickles the bristles were generously brushing my privates with, and the tail end of my vertebra was grinding painfully against the elephant's backbone.

Impervious to my suffering, the elephant marched resolutely on, barely clearing the low-hanging branches of the coniferous trees along the narrow road. My heavy Santa padding prevented me from bending to avoid overhead branches and I began slipping down the side of the elephant. The mahouts appeared not to realise that something was wrong, merely stopping at intervals to prop me back upright. When Santa finally arrived at the club after the ride of a lifetime, he was hanging for dear life onto the stomach of the pachyderm. The waiting crowd at the club were roaring with laughter

SANTA SETS OUT FOR THE PARTY.

137

and the mahouts had a tough time rescuing Santa, by now practically comatose in his agony.

In later years when I climbed on the back of an elephant on safaris in Kenya and Kaziranga, it was always to ride on a bench placed there, and I would remember the foolhardy glory of my younger days when I rode bareback on an elephant and lived to tell the tale!

The children's Christmas party at the Anamallai Club, 1985. Santa, having survived the ordeal, is seen collapsed against the wall by the tree.

THE HISTORY OF THE CULTIVATION OF TEA

Madras District Gazetteers, The Nilgiris, **Volume I by W Francis, Madras (1908) p178-182**

The history of the cultivation of tea in the district dates from 1833. Assistant-Surgeon Christie had noticed that a Camelia, which was known to resemble its cousin the tea-plant in its tastes, grew abundantly near Coonoor, and he therefore ordered some tea-plants from China. He died before they arrived, but the plants were distributed to various parts of the hills for trial . In 1835 some plants raised from seed brought from China by the secretary of a committee appointed by the then Governor-General to consider means to introduce tea-cultivation in India were sent from Calcutta to the Nilgiris - and also to Coorg, Mysore and Madras. Those sent to the Nilgiris were chiefly planted out at the Keti experimental farm referred to below. When this was closed in 1886 and its buildings were lent to the Governor of Pondicherry as a residence (see p. 331), M. Perrottet the French botanist found that the plants had

A TEA PLUCKER IN THE NILGIRIS.
IMAGE FROM TEA BOARD INDIA C1980S.

G.E.C.
electrical equipment

for tea estates

G. E. C. is in a position to carry out complete electri-
fication schemes for tea factories, and supply Industrial
Fans, Lighting, and Fittings etc.

For further particulars please write to :-
THE GENERAL ELECTRIC CO. OF INDIA PRIVATE LTD.
Representing : THE GENERAL ELECTRIC CO. LTD. OF ENGLAND

FROM *PLANTING DIRECTORY OF SOUTHERN INDIA*, UPASI, COONOOR (1956)

been half-buried by ignorant gardeners and were consequently in a very bad state. He uncovered them and cared for them, and in October 1838 they had grown to four feet in height and were loaded with flowers, fruit and healthy young leaves. He published an account of them which attracted attention and in 1840 samples of Nilgiri tea made from plants growing at Keti and Billikal were sent by Mr. J. Sullivan to the Madras Agri-horticultural Society. The leaves had been withered in the open and fired in a frying-pan for want of better means, but the tea was pronounced excellent by the enthusiasts who tasted it .

Later Mr. Mann of Coonoor succeeded in making really fair tea from the Nilgiri plants and was thus encouraged to get more seed. He procured a supply from the finest plantations in China early in 1851, and after many difficulties put them down in the piece of land near Coonoor which is now known as the Coonoor Tea Estate. As early as 1856 the tea made from these plants was favourably reported upon by the London brokers, but Mr. Mann was so disheartened by the difficulty of procuring forest land to extend his operations that he eventually gave up the experiment.

Dr. Cleghorn, Conservator of Forests, noticed later on how well the trees were seeding and endeavoured to induce Government to form a nursery from this seed and to import a trained Chinese tea-maker or two from the North-West Provinces. But Sir Charles Trevelyan, then Governor of Madras, in a characteristic minute strongly deprecated State intervention in the matter and the 'morbid habit of dependence upon Government, which in some communities has amounted to a moral paralysis.'

DRINK

K.T.E.

TEA

Famous for its exquisite delicacy of flavour and aroma. It appeals to the most critical tastes. The following list of awards will show how it is appreciated by the highest judges :

Five First Prizes,
Eight Silver Medals,
Three Gold Medals and Diplomas,
Three Bronze Medals and Seven Diplomas nd First Class Certificate.

Sole Wholesale Agents :

SPENCER & Co., Ltd., (MADRAS.)

BOMBAY, 77-89, ARGYLE ROAD.
Branch : HORNBY ROAD, FORT.

An advertisement for tea from Kodanad Estate (near Kotagiri) in *Times of India* on 20 April 1910.

From Saaz's album.

About the same time as Mr. Mann formed his plantation at Coonoor, Mr. Kao obtained a grant of land near Sholur, now known as the Dunsandle Estate, for growing tea; shortly afterwards a garden was begun at Kotagiri; and in 1863 the estate known as Belmont was formed on the Bishopsdown property at Ootacamund.

During Sir William Denison's governorship some direct aid was afforded to the new industry in 1863 and 1864 by bringing down tea-makers from the North-West Provinces, distributing gratuitously a stock of seed also obtained from thence, and forming a small nursery within the cinchona plantations at Dodabetta; but none of these steps affected much good and the tea planters worked out their own salvation by their own energy.

By the end of 1800, some 200 or so acres had been planted with tea and at the Ootacamund agricultural exhibition in that year no less than eighteen planters showed samples of their produce. At the suggestion of Mr. Breeks, Commissioner of the Nilgiris, some of these were sent Home by Government for the opinion of the brokers, and many of them were pronounced good and some very good, their value ranging from 1s. 4d. to 6s.

MARSHALLS
"Quality"

TEA DRYING MACHINE

Available in 3 ft., 4 ft. and 6 ft. sizes, these modern machines are designed to bring out the highest quality in the teas produced. High output is combined with very low working and maintenance costs.

STOCKS HELD IN MADRAS

MARSHALL, SONS & CO. (INDIA) LTD.,
MARSHALL'S BUILDING,
9-SECOND LINE BEACH, MADRAS-1.

FROM *PLANTING DIRECTORY OF SOUTHERN INDIA*, UPASI, COONOOR (1956)

per pound.

Since then the output has steadily increased year by year, notwithstanding a corresponding gradual decrease in the prices realized, which are now less than half what they were in the seventies.

Efforts are being made to create a market for tea among natives of India, which, if established, would free the growers from the heavy middlemen's charges which absorb so much of the profits on this and other produce disposed of through Mincing Lane.

From the 1st April 1903 a compulsory customs cess of one quarter of a pie per pound on all tea exported from India was imposed by law and the proceeds of this are handed over to a Tea Cess Special Committee to be expended in pushing the sale and increasing the consumption of tea outside the United Kingdom.

PROCESSES OF MANUFACTURE

The tea plant is botanically a Camelia, and its blossom closely resembles that of the ordinary single white Camelia and has a similar scent. Three varieties are grown. First there is the pure China tea, the chief merit of which is its hardiness; then, the indigenous Assam sort, which in its natural habitat is a forest tree growing to a height of 25 or 30 feet; and lastly the hybrid between these two, which is the most useful and generally grown of the three. This produces twice as much, leaf as the pure China, and yet possesses a great deal of the latter's hardiness.

The cultivation and manufacture of tea are subjects on which much has been written and the details of which are quite outside the scope of this present volume. A few words may however be said regarding the processes through which the leaf passes from the time when it is plucked until it is duly packed in its lead-lined chest.

Each of the leaves of the shoot of a tea plant is known by a technical name. The bud at the extreme end is called the tip or flowery pekoe; the two next to it orange pekoe; the two next, souchong; and the next two, the largest of the series, congou. When a 'flush' or burst of young green leaf, occurs on the estate these (or, if 'fine plucking' is required, the bud and the first two) are all plucked together by women and children. They are not kept separately then, but are sifted afterwards by machinery. The leaves are plucked into baskets and carried the same day to the tea factory. Unlike coffee, tea cannot be partly manufactured on the estate and partly afterwards elsewhere, and every plantation must therefore either possess its own tea-making plant or be near enough to some other estate which is equipped with the necessary machinery and is willing to make a neighbour's leaf into tea for a consideration. Thus much outlay in buildings and machinery is usually required for starting a tea-estate; and tea-planting has the further disadvantage when compared with coffee-growing that manufacture is going on almost all the year round; whereas the coffee-planter enjoys comparative peace and quiet except at that one period of the year when his crop is coming in.

Having been taken to the tea-house, the leaf is 'withered' by being spread thinly on shelves of some material and left there, until it can be rolled between the fingers without breaking. Like almost every other process in tea-making, this stage requires to be

"Sirocco" Dust Removal Plant in a
Tea Factory

Whether the problem involves moving of volumes of air or creating warmth and comfort over large areas or removing fumes or hot gases from industrial processes, extracting foul air from offices or exhausting dust, or providing draught for cupolas or furnaces or the hundred and one problems.

You can depend on :

"SIROCCO" FANS

Agents in South India :

Harrisons & Crosfield Ltd.

(Incorporated in England—Liability of Members Limited)

QUILON

FROM PLANTING DIRECTORY OF SOUTHERN INDIA, UPASI, COONOOR (1956)

timed with care and experience. If the leaf is not sufficiently withered it will break when 'rolled' as described below, while if it is left to wither too long the quality of the 'liquor' made from it is inferior.

When the withering is complete the leaf is taken to be rolled. This is done in machines consisting of two horizontal brass-faced plates placed one above the other like the stones in a mill, which are rapidly revolved by steam with an eccentric motion. This rolling, again, requires to be timed to a nicety or subsequent processes are adversely affected. The smaller leaves naturally roll quickest, so to secure evenness in the rolling and subsequent fermenting (see below) the leaf is next usually sifted and the bigger leaf rolled a second time. When the rolling is complete the leaf is laid out in a thin layer in a darkened and moist room and left to ferment. This process requires perhaps more careful watching than any other, the time required to complete it differing with the size of the leaf, the elevation, and the humidity mid warmth of the atmosphere. The point at which the process is complete is judged partly by the smell, and partly by the colour, of the leaf. It should be a bright copper colour. The moment this stage has arrived fermentation must be stopped by 'firing', or roasting the leaf. This is effected by scattering it in very thin layers on shallow wire trays and placing the latter, in a machine called a 'sirocco' in which hot air from a charcoal fire is drawn over and between the trays by a fan. This firing changes the leaf into the usual black tea of the shops. This operation again requires extreme care. Any tea which has been burnt by overfiring makes a bitter 'liquor,' and unless the overfiring is detected at once before the spoilt leaf is mixed with the rest of the 'break' a few ounces of this overfired leaf will ruin the flavour of many pounds of good tea.

Next, the fired tea is sifted by machinery. Different estates make different grades of tea, but the classes usually distinguished are orange pekoe, broken pekoe, pekoe, pekoe souchong, broken souchong and congou, which are named from the nature of the leaves (see above) of which they consist. The largest leaves are then broken in a special machine which cuts them into neat pieces.

The tea is finally stored in bins until it is ready to be packed. To make sure that it is absolutely dry and will not get musty in transit, it is generally given a final firing just before being placed in its lead-lined chest. Well-equipped tea-factories possess an ingenious machine for packing. This consists of a little table, big enough to carry a chest, which is vibrated rapidly by machinery. The chest is placed on this and the vibrations shake the tea evenly and tightly down into all the corners.

BABA BOODEN

Excerpted from *Madras District Gazetteers, The Nilgiris,* Volume I by W Francis, Madras (1908) p170

According to tradition, the coffee-plant was introduced into Mysore by a Muhammadan pilgrim named Baba Booden who came and took up his abode in the uninhabited range now known as the Baba Booden hills, where he established a kind of college. It is said that he brought with him from Mocha seven coffee berries, which lie planted near his hermitage. Some very old coffee trees still stand in this area.

A COFFEE PLANTATION, CHIKMAGALUR, 2008.
ORIGINAL PHOTOGRAPH BY KANCHANA SUNDERARAJAN

BEARING IN MIND THAT COFFEE CAME FIRST

From the original planting in Baba Budangiri, Chikmagalur, coffee plants thrived and soon became native to the area, with plantations extending into the hilly tracts of the Western Ghats. Closely following the blossom showers, millions of flowers open, draping entire bushes in white finery reminiscent of a richly-embroidered bridal gown. Swarms of bees are attracted by their fragrance, and honey emerges as an important offering of the Coorg economy. The cool and moist ecosystems provided by the tall shade trees make coffee estates an ideal abode for animals like elephants, bison, sambars, langurs, macaques, civet cats, and Malabar squirrels, in addition to a host of birds.

Although the hills of South India are lush with plantations which produce a range of crops including spices of various kinds, rubber, coffee and tea, most of these are grown at low altitudes and tea thrives higher up, with the best bouquet from plantations situated at 3500 to 8000 feet. And therefore, there was very little social interaction between tea and coffee planters. The crops too require different management, agro-climatic conditions, cultural practices and skills. Even propagation varies: tea depends almost entirely on the vegetative growth of the tea bush, while coffee seeds are a product of coffee blossoms, cross-pollinated by bees and butterflies to produce white flowers that bear berries which ripen into purple fruit enclosing the seeds that are collected to be pulped, roasted and ground and produce coffee brew.

Life on Manamboly was paradise for Rajkumar Wilson and his wife Rani. He was manager of this large coffee estate in the Anamallais, and we loved visiting them on Sundays and picnicking in a scenic spot by the river. Paradise, that is, until an electric fence was installed around the estate boundaries to prevent damage caused by wild animals. Little did the management realise that a number of animals, including a pair of bison, had actually been impounded in the process within the fenced property.

Work on the estate became difficult as the startled animals, which were not used to confinement, detested their captivity and ran amuck. Gaurs charged on workers as they went about their daily tasks and though the workers tried to defend themselves, they were no match for the wild animals. In a few short days, cultivation work on the estate stopped completely. Declaring a truce, the management dismantled the electric fence and the animals were left to wander about at free will. Nature followed its course and in time the bison couple produced a calf, further glorifying the romance of coffee.

WOUNDED PANTHER

Tea Estates India, owned by Brooke Bond, was among the first to enter the Anamallais and pick the gently rolling hills around the villages of Rottikadai and Valparai, to demarcate five tea estates interspersed with swamps, streams, roads and ravines. Sirikundra, the first, was started in 1898, and the bulk of the plantings were done over the next twenty-five years. During this time, a newly-formed township developed as the taluka headquarters and adopted the name Valparai. Two of the five estates, Nullacathu and Stanmore, were situated around this town while Monica, Injipara and Sirikundra adjoined the two original villages, and together they formed the Stanmore Group.

Blessed with dependable monsoons and tropical sun, the virgin soil provided ideal conditions for tea plantations that transformed the hill ranges to endless carpets of green. Injipara, located in this delightful setting and with a well-regarded factory and a huge bungalow with a swimming pool, tennis court and sprawling gardens, was a coveted posting awarded to expatriates or senior managers, and I was fortunate to be appointed to the position in 1984, the same year in which Brooke Bond was acquired by Unilever.

The estate bungalow had been built by the British in 1935, nearly fifty years before it became my family's home. Among the trees in the orchard were jackfruit,

FANTAIL IN A NEST WITH ITS
BABIES, UNDER A TEA BUSH
ORIGINAL PHOTO BY KUNTAL DESAI

papaya, lychee and avocado, and these provided a leafy sanctuary to flocks of various birds which became rather noisy, with crows dominating, in the fruit-bearing season. We feasted on the fruit and distributed large quantities, but I must mention that it was the parrots who always helped themselves to the best ripe lychees!

The climate of Injipara was conducive and provided refuge to a host of wild animals that continued to live in their natural habitat despite the significant and growing human presence. As a result, animal sightings were quite common. However, there are some animals which, even when a large population is present, remain unseen. We were privileged while returning to the bungalow late one evening, to see in the bright headlights, a full-grown panther limping just ahead of our car. The poor animal's right forepaw was badly hurt, doubtless while trying to extricate it from a poacher's snare. It continued to limp along while we trailed behind. After a short while, we were astonished to see it suddenly lie on a lump of cow dung on the road, roll all over it, finishing with a thorough face-rub, after which it turned and faced the car, baring its teeth and snarling. The poor creature, in no condition to hunt, fight or flee, had taken measures to disguise its smell and camouflage its tracks, and was now putting on a brave front. We turned away respectfully, feeling sorry and hoping that it would soon be healed.

On another occasion, we were woken at midnight by loud conversation, and were surprised to see the estate field officer in an animated discussion with a few workmen in the dimly-lit porch. Stepping out, we were aghast to be confronted with a huge dead panther, its face fixed in a majestic grimace, laid full length on the ground. The animal was still warm and it was disconcerting to see the end of its tail appearing to twitch at intervals, bringing a shiver to all of us standing there every time it happened. I was informed that one of the estate tractors had been transporting compost. Immediately after the engine of the tractor passed, the unsuspecting carnivore had tried to leap across the road, only to be run over by the solid metal trailer the tractor was towing, and was instantly killed. The traumatised workers who had seen this happen raced to wake up the field officer, and they had together brought the dead creature to my home.

It was a terrible thing to have killed a panther, even accidentally, not least because the wildlife laws were strict and it would be assumed that a crime had been committed until proved otherwise. The field officer devised an ingenious plan and had the carcass transported to the main road, and left at a junction that was shared by three estates, Injipara, Senguthupara (a division of Monica), and Korangumudi. This made it hard – impossible – to assign blame precisely. The government machinery arrived at the site next morning in full force. At the inquest, the veterinary surgeon found flies swarming around the panther's ear, where blood had clotted. This led the vet to believe that the panther must have had something wrong with its ear. After due deliberation, he pronounced the cause of death to be consequent to an 'ear infection'. The carcass was given a duly respectful burial.

My tea man

The tea man, my companion and mascot for more than half a century, has had an interesting, if sedentary life. He has usually resided on the front porch of my bungalow. When people entered, they would inquire about what he represented. A crucifix, perhaps? Or the image of a toiling plantation worker? Or the genesis of a modern superhero? Or an artistic umbrella stand? It is a story I am always happy to tell.

A tea plant, left to nature, grows to a height of twenty feet or more. Its beautiful white blossoms resemble those

V Ramaswamy, the tea man, KS Medappa and Nana Menon pose together in the Woodbrook garden, sporting antique hats Nana purchased at a clearance sale at Bailey Brothers, a store next to Shinkows, which was closing down as it no longer had customers for its products. Woodbrook, 1968.
Image courtesy KS Medappa

of the camellia, and have a refreshing fragrance. For the purpose of commercial cultivation, tea bushes are kept low by periodical pruning, and maintained at a height of four feet to form an optimum plucking table. Such tea bushes, nurtured well, are known to live and share their bounty for even over a hundred years.

When I first came across my tea man, he was in fact a fully-grown tea tree in one of the wind belts of Prospect, in 1968.

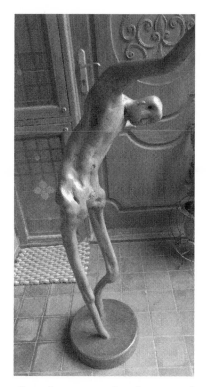

Two erect stems grew out of a clump at the base and through the mass of its branches and roots, it took some imagination to perceive the human form. The artistic skills of carpenter Shekaran did the rest.

Ever since, the tea man .has been my companion, a mute witness to my journey of life. Quite unfortunately, my tea man had a limb amputated from the left elbow at a party at my home, when a friend got roaring drunk and took a swipe at him with a pruning knife.

I leave you to decide what he represents. But whatever he represents, he was never an umbrella stand. He deserves respect.

The marvels of technology

A fond memory, from Victor Dey

At the Seaforth factory, we used an ingenious contraption to generate electricity, a Pelton Wheel. It was a large circular etched disc that extracted energy from falling water. It's amazing to think of how this was built by the pioneers who constructed Seaforth, which was still a wilderness when I worked there a hundred years later.

A river ran past Seaforth, and a canal had been dug from the entrance of the estate to the Seaforth hospital and stored in a tank nearby. From there it flowed through large pipes onto the Pelton Wheel in the factory five or six hundred feet below. The force of the water on the wheel generated electricity on which the factory machines worked. The main electric line from the grid was erratic and the Pelton Wheel supported quite a lot of the factory's production.

SEAFORTH ESTATE, WITH THE FACTORY SEEN IN THE DISTANCE.
ORIGINAL PHOTOGRAPH BY CAROLYN HOLLIS

Power supply from the main grid was from Pykara, and it was prone to disruption for various reasons. All tea factories had standby power, and the Pelton Wheel at Seaforth powered a 52.5 KV generator. Given the copious water supply in those days, it was the ideal standby for the Seaforth factory. In 1970, for the first time we experienced a 100 percent

IMAGE OF A PELTON
WHEEL

power cut in Tamil Nadu. The Pelton wasn't working at the time. Mr NSV Sinniah, who was very inventive, came up with a solution and we ran some of the machinery on tractors. We used the grid of pulleys the factory was installed with for the Pelton Wheel, to generate and transfer power from the main shaft to the machine part that had to be moved.

THE OLD E&A GANG AT BANGALORE CLUB: RAM ADIGE, KS
MEDAPPA, RAVINDRAN, VICTOR DEY, NANA MENON AND CYRUS
LALKAKA, DURING NANA'S VISIT TO INDIA IN JAN 2016.

LABOUR AT WORK ON A CEYLON TEA PLANTATION. ABOVE, WOMEN
PLUCK TEA LEAVES, AND BELOW, MEN PRUNE TEA BUSHES.
FROM *GOLDEN TIPS. A DESCRIPTION OF CEYLON AND ITS GREAT TEA INDUSTRY*,
HENRY W CAVE, LONDON (1904) P153 & 154

A time that once was

Senthil Chengalvarayan talks about his father, NSV Sinniah, and his memories of life on the tea estates.

My father left his village in Ramnad District in South India when he was seven years old. His father had just died, and he was sent to Ceylon to live with his older cousin Savumiamoorthy Thondaman. Thondaman was the leader of the Indian Tamils in Ceylon and his father had been the first non-white to own tea estates in the country. Thondaman and his wife Kodhai took my father to Nuwara Eliya, where they brought him up with great affection. My dad completed his education at St Anthony's in Kandy and took up a job managing Meddagoda, one of Thondaman's many tea estates, in 1950.

My parents were married in 1951 and I was born in 1963. Even in the early 1960s, my father had a sense that Tamils were not welcome in Ceylon and decided, probably against his cousin's wishes, to return to India. He sought the help of a friend of his, David Hacking, who had moved from Sri Lanka to Coonoor in the Nilgiris. With Hacking's help, my father got a job on Terrace Estate and moved there in 1964. My parents decided that my mother would stay on with me in Ceylon until he was settled.

Terrace was owned by the Maharaja of Mysore and managed by Matheson Bosanquet, and my father was its first Indian manager. Terrace was wild and beautiful, the highest estate in the Nilgiris. It was at the top of a very steep hill, and our old Herald would struggle to climb up in first gear.

It was so cold in Terrace that when my dad sat by the fireplace to write, the side of his face facing the fire would be warm but the other side would keep getting colder and he would have to keep changing his position, turning to stay uniformly warm! The wind was so strong that the trees near the bungalow were stunted. Water froze in the pipes at night. My father missed the camaraderie of the plantations of Ceylon. The evenings were especially miserable. Then one day, he received a letter inviting him to Sunday lunch at the home of a neighbour, Krishnakutty, who lived a mere ninety-minute drive away! It was a treat to look forward to – till my father noticed that the letter had reached him a week late – on the Monday after the lunch! He was dismayed to have missed the opportunity for company and a meal with others, and his teamaker Mukundan, who was related to the Krishnakuttys, kindly advised him to present himself for lunch the following Sunday, which he did. This was the start of a very close friendship and a series of Sunday lunches at their home.

The Krishnakuttys, who owned Woodbriar Estate near Gudalur, were much older than my father, and he called them Amma and Appa. Mr Krishnakutty was keen that my father work with him, but my father declined as he did not want their relationship to change. But the visits continued. I remember going to their bungalow for lunches and being fascinated by their futuristic gobar – cow dung – gas plant. It was the first gas stove I saw, as estate bungalow kitchens in those days used ancient wood-fired Aga stoves.

Years later, my dad dreamt that Mr Krishnakutty was on his deathbad. As soon as he woke up, he telephoned Mr Krishnakutty's son Rajaram to ask after his father, only to be told that the old man had just passed away. That was the kind of connection the two of them had.

My early childhood was spent at Terrace and I loved it there. While most planters' wives had huge adjustment issues, my mother Visalakshi, who was the daughter of a planter, took to life in the Nilgiris much more easily.

In 1968, we moved to Seaforth Estate, which was at a lower altitude and deep in the jungle. The road from Gudalur turned into a mud track all the way to O Valley, past Glenvans estate, to Seaforth. After Yellamalai division, it was nothing but jungle with the Kerala border beyond. One time, my dad and his colleague Victor Dey were driving back from the O Valley Club when they saw a cloud of dust ahead of them. Victor suggested driving faster to catch up with whoever it was – but they soon discovered that it wasn't a car they were chasing but a running elephant!

My Dad would spot elephants almost every time he'd drive back home from the club, but somehow never when my mother was with him. She would always complain about that. Once when they were returning home, she finally saw an elephant climbing the hillside. But it began slipping down! As they raced away, my mother decided that she no longer minded not seeing elephants.

Another time, legend has it, one of the Wapshares fell into an elephant pit. These pits, covered with dry grass, were dug to trap wild elephants and were not deep or spiked; they were meant only to capture the elephant and not to harm it. It would then be trained by tame elephants and join the workforce for logging, transporting, and perhaps also temple duty. Wapshare was rescued after a day or two in the pit, and must have heaved a sigh of relief. What if an elephant had fallen in on top of him!

As one of the earliest Indian managers in Ceylon as well as in India, my father worked with British planters and one of the things he used to say was that they were mindful of spending and particular about keeping accounts. There is a stereotype about Scots being stingy, but my dad believed they were just being careful because they had to fend for themselves and save for their retirement as they did not have the kind of safety net that Indian families give their members.

Taking over from British managers, my father was well known for two major contributions. One, his teas would always get very good prices. And two, he worked continuously to eliminate wastage. The Seaforth factory was the first to be brought to zero wastage. He used simple, common-sense engineering to improve the quality of tea. I remember one of his most obvious innovations – getting the channels that ran alongside the rubber conveyor belts, which carried the crushed green tea leaves, cleaned. He ensured that the leaves that fell off the belt and into the channels were put back onto the belt. No one had paid attention to this before, and the leaves had been allowed to lie in the channels for days, where they fermented. Now fewer fresh leaves were

RAM ADIGE, CYRUS LALKAKA, DAVID HOLLIS, NSV SINNIAH
IMAGES COURTESY ABHIRAMI SHANKAR

wasted, and the fermented and rotting leaves were removed. Taste improved, and prices increased.

When my father first joined Seaforth, a chunk of the estate land was being used by the labour to grow ginger, which they sold for high prices. He got it all pulled out, despite his predecessor

WITH MY PARENTS AND YOUNGER SISTER, ABHIRAMI. SEAFORTH, 1969

warning him it could get him killed. He wasn't killed but was certainly unpopular for a while. I remember the strikes he faced. Once when I was sitting alone in the car I was gheraoed – surrounded to intimidate – by a large group of men and women workers. When my father walked out of his office and saw what was going on, he shouted loudly asking what kind of human beings would do this to a child, strode angrily through the crowd of gheraoing workers to the car, opened the door and drove off, giving it an extra growling rev for effect.

Despite such occasional run-ins, the staff had huge respect and affection for my dad. I remember that in Terrace where it was bitterly cold, he would drive the cook and helpers home if we had a late dinner. It was this empathy that endeared him to the people he worked with, even if he took tough and unpopular decisions at times. By the time we left Seaforth, they had grown very fond of him. Knowing that he'd accept no farewell gift, the predominantly Muslim staff gave him something the devout Hindu could not refuse – a 9-inch bronze statue of Lord Murugan! We still have the statue.

JINI DEY, KS MEDAPPA AND MY
PARENTS WITH ABHIRAMI AT OUR
FAREWELL FROM SEAFORTH IN 1972.

On Terrace we had a designated rat catcher. At Seaforth the rats were taken care of by snakes, so we had a snake catcher instead. Any worker who caught a snake could bring it to the office and receive payment. (Its head would be chopped off so that they couldn't take it away and bring it back for another claim!)

One day Brown, the chief mechanic, found a python in the office and came to our house, took my father's double-barrel shotgun and shot it. Another time he shot a king cobra. Those skins lay around the house until one day when our friends Bob and Situ Savur came to visit. We gave them to Situ Aunty and she took them with her on her next trip to Bombay where she got two handbags and a wallet made, so those snakes remained with us for a while longer!

Our life on the plantations was lavish and fulfilling in many ways. But when I completed my education and decided that this was going to be the life for me and was offered a job on an estate in the Nilgiris, my dad put his foot down. He had never before tried to stop me from doing anything that I wanted to do but this time he was firm. He could clearly see that the glamour and privileges of a planter's life had no place in the world to come. He could see that the glory days were gone for good, and we were among the fortunate few to have experienced them.

WHY NOT WYNAAD

The Wynaad and The Planting Industry of Southern India, by Francis Ford, Madras (1895) piv

It must be borne in mind that the Wynaad is admittedly as favourable as Ceylon in respect to climate, soil and distribution of rainfall ; it is far superior to both that Island and Assam as regards a cheap labour supply ; and again, if we except the more favoured districts of Ceylon, in regard to cheap transport and proximity to the sea-board. A good trunk-road, at present kept up by Imperial funds for military reasons, runs through the district ; from the head of the ghaut to the Calicut Custom house the distance is only thirty-nine miles, and there is an excellent cheap cart service between the coast and the hills.

The planter's life offers for a youngster with a small capital greater attractions possibly than any other. Good climate, good sport, good friends and good prospects are all here ; and if at the end fortune does not crown him, he will at any rate be able to look back on a career full of happy hours, staunch friendships and jovial reminiscences. There is not a community in the world that has stronger esprit de corps than the planters of the tropics. Goodwill and kind-heartedness abound: hospitality with them is almost a fault. A grumbler at trifles and passing cares the planter is, but let reverses come, trials that test the mettle of the heart, and no man will bear them more lightly and bravely. With gangs of labourers working on his plantation, servants round the house at his beck and call, with horse in stable, dogs in kennel, and gun and rifle on the rack, he lives in quaint baronial style, himself a very parody of an English country gentleman, one of the olden times.

An unforgettable New Year's Eve

Contributed by Arjun Ravindran, based on his memories as a ten-year-old

This story starts, as all overly-dramatized ones do, on a dark and stormy night. The parents were getting ready, preparing to leave the manse in the capable but tremulous hands of their ten-year-old.

"We'll be back in the morning when you've woken up, and you can wish us Happy New Year!" they chirped, as they got into the car. "And don't forget, if you need anything, Velu is just a bell-press away," Velu being the resident cook who was more like a member of the family.

After having dinner, the children settled in for the night, eager to watch the Doordarshan New Year's Eve countdown, drift off happily to sleep and await the dawning of the New Year and its unlimited promise. Little did they know that what was in store was a thrilling evening that would be the most exciting one they would have for many years to come.

It started very quietly. Almost too quiet to notice, a low moan came through the bedroom curtains. "Ah, it must be the wind," thought the ten-year-old. It had just started drizzling a little earlier, and a lashing of rain seemed likely. The TV program droned on in the background. Soon the moan took on a distinctly animal tone. "Hmm," thought the ten-year-old, "I wonder what that was!" And he turned up the TV volume.

"Did you hear that?" inquired the seven-year-old, "What was that sound?" And with those short questions, the noise and the menace that could have been denied had become undeniably real. "Oh don't worry about it," he told his little sister confidently. "It's just the wind." But even as the words left his mouth he felt doubt creep in, and knew that his sister's eyes were fixed to the back of his head while he stared at the TV bravely attempting to appear nonchalant.

"Gulp!" he thought, in the manner of a character in the comic books he was accustomed to devouring, "What do I do now?" He surreptitiously pushed the bell-press, hoping that Velu would come along and allay their fears. After all, nothing sinister had ever happened here, no matter what the ghost stories said.

There was no response to the first bell-press. "Maybe he didn't hear it, I'll press it again," announced the ten-year-old. No one had asked, but the sound of his own voice reassured him that all was still well.

A more insistent bell-press, filled with conviction and need; still no response. At this point the noise had waned, and just as he had begun feeling a little more hopeful, an unmistakable shriek pierced the air. The two pulled the blanket over their heads, their bravado flowing away like so many raindrops sliding down the windowpane.

The shrieking, screaming noise waxed and waned sometimes appearing to be right outside the window (later they found out, it was) and sometimes so far away as to blend in with the moaning wind. It conjured up the most unspeakable terrors imaginable, as if a demon had escaped the fires of hell and come back to haunt the living, or a roomful of children was being ripped apart by a beast with ten-thousand teeth and claws.

The bell-press was now welded to his hand, clenched and permanently pressed, as if that would keep the terror away. What was worse was that he could now clearly hear the bell ring as well, and he knew that the bell was working. "What could have happened to Velu?" he thought feverishly, "Maybe the monster got him and is coming for us now?" The possibility of facing this creature unarmed filled him with dread. He needed a weapon, any weapon to go down fighting, to defend his sister, who had fallen asleep as if nothing was the matter.

Clutching his father's pocketknife, with a blade no more than a couple of inches long, and a spring-loaded action that was so tight that he was never actually going to be able to use it, he crawled out from under the covers, determined to make his last stand at the bedroom door. As he slowly opened the bedroom door and peered out, looking down the long unlit corridor, the loudest shriek shredded the night and woke his sister, who burst out crying.

Slamming the bedroom door shut, he ran back to the bed, where they both dived headfirst into the covers, and lay there motionless, except for the slight trembling that they could not control.

And it was like this that their parents discovered them the next morning, sleeping with their heads under the covers, the puny pocketknife still clutched tight in the ten-year-old's hand. "Happy New Year!" they announced.

The practitioner of witchcraft

Pitchaimuthu, who ran the estate canteen on a lease, was a sub-committee member of the ruling party and had influence over the political establishment, including the local police and government authorities. Calling in favours from key officials, he was able to engage in the illicit sale of alcohol, a flourishing underground business due to Prohibition in the state. This business put him at loggerheads with every manager of the estates as he knew precisely whom among the workers were most vulnerable and, as his business depended on them, he worked hard and systematically to fuel their addiction and alcoholism.

Pitchaimuthu was also a practitioner of witchcraft and had a following of unhappy people including childless couples, disgruntled workers, those with incurable diseases, and others who enjoyed creating trouble. He also used 'black magic' as a tool to terrorise the estate management.

The entrance to the bungalow where we lived had a massive Spathodia tree, a tree known to grow up to 80 feet. Its bright red flowers formed a copious red carpet around it when they fell. At the base of the tree were several spears driven into it by worshippers. Large conical stones anointed with vermilion stood around it. Offerings of milk, banana and eggs had resulted in ant hills, and visits by snakes were not uncommon.

On chosen nights, mostly Fridays, Pitchaimuthu would get drunk and come with a noisy crowd of followers, holding a cockerel donated by one of them, and loudly chanting incoherent mumbo jumbo that masqueraded as slokas – Vedic verses.

After lighting several mud lamps and incense sticks, and feverishly ringing a bell, he would scream loudly and bite the live chicken's head off. In a frenzy, he would then pin the writhing bird on the spear and let its blood flow to the ground.

When the crowd dispersed, satisfied with the offerings and prayers, Pitchaimuthu would race down in the darkness to an isolated place by the river where he was building a shrine. There, the childless couple who had been asked to be present would be waiting in reverence for the godman's orders for his personalised worship ceremony.

On that fateful day, frustrated that the management was ignoring the continuous noise and nuisance he was staging at the entrance to the bungalow, Pitchaimuthu decided to take the war inside and came right to the front door to terrorise our children, who were home for their Christmas vacation.

One of the great handicaps of plantation life is the physical distance from good-quality schools. Most planters either sent their children to be boarders at one of the reputed schools in nearby hill stations, or to live with family members in their hometowns, as we did. Either way, the children would only come home during their vacations. When Rajam and I went to the club in the evenings, the children would be left in the care of

Sainaba, an elderly Mopla woman. This was the first time we had left Velu in charge, as Sainaba was unwell. The villainous Pitchaimuthu had chosen the interval at which Velu went to have his meal (at the home of Armugham, our cusni-matey – kitchen help, cusni being the Nilgiri Tamil word for kitchen – who lived nearby), to conduct his high-pitched, terrifying sorcery.

Next morning, the police found four eggs, one in each corner of the compound, with my name written on them in Tamil with a lead pencil. Here was evidence of an act of 'black magic'! We filed a police complaint and Pitchaimuthu was called to the station and given a warning. This put a pause to his dream of building a hut by the river to conduct his disreputable activities. Or perhaps he kept trying and eventually did succeed in doing so!

OUR MULTI-CULTURAL LAND

While the managers of our tea estates were a rich mix of people from different communities across the country, our labour force, who were recruited right since inception in groups from their villages, were from three southern states. Mostly they were Tamils from the southern part of Tamil Nadu; in the Anamallais they came from nearby Coimbatore; in some parts of the Nilgiris and Wynaad they were from Karnataka. They were mostly Hindu but many estates had Christians and churches were built for them. In the Nilgiri-Wynaad area around Gudalur and the northern districts of Kerala, there was a large percentage of Mopla workers who followed Islam. Mosques had been built on those estates and the muezzin's call to prayers was a familiar sound five times a day. On Fridays, work would stop at noon for the men to go to the mosque. Each one practised their religion and celebrated their festivals unhindered. It did happen occasionally that when a procession passed the place of worship of another faith, a skirmish would break out, leading to tension and lawlessness. Suryanarayanan, manager of Rockwood Estate, once faced an extremely tense situation that he handled tactfully, averting a potentially dangerous communal outburst. But such events were rare and life was mostly peaceful.

Entry of Syrian Christians into the plantation industry

Edited extracts from the paper *Rise of the indigenous elite around Travancore* presented by Emil Manu Oommen at International Conference on Indian Business & Economic History, Indian Institute of Management, Ahmedabad (IIMA), August 2019.

In the late eighteenth century, the princely state of Travancore had a densely populated pluri-religious society in which Syrian Christians emerged as a significant group because of their economic and educational advancements. In the early nineteenth century, the kingdom became a protectorate of the British Empire, and there was a protest from the educated middle class belonging to various religious communities of Travancore, criticising the discriminatory attitude of the government in appointing Tamil Brahmins to government service. In 1891, a memorandum known as Malayali Memorial documented this unrest and was presented to the court, and this opened the way for recruitment from different communities. This gave Syrian Christians too the opportunity to advance as one of the progressive communities of Kerala.

Syrian Christians are seen historically as more entrepreneurial, particularly in the context of the disdain in which some other upwardly-mobile communities viewed trading activities at the time. The Syrian Christian laws of inheritance, in which land became the sole share of proprietary rights, enabled individuals to receive large sums as loans to pursue their entrepreneurial ambitions. These financial resources led to the establishment of banks by Syrian Christians, which in turn enabled members of the community to invest in plantations, and they prospered in both sectors.

Between 1905 and 1910, the newly-established newspaper Malayala Manorama wrote thirteen editorials on the plantations, postulating that the fertile land of Travancore belonged to the Travancorians; criticising the acquisition of large tracts by Europeans and the massive profits they generated; the negligence of the crown in not promoting the cultivation of cash crops among the natives; and instigating natives to be more enterprising. Rubber production intensified during the years of the First World War and then the Second World War, and this stimulated the growth of the Travancore economy. Malayala Manorama continued to document the growing prosperity of individual planters, attracting well-off natives to aspire to own plantations too.

Malayalis were known to have leftist leanings and planters preferred to recruit a non-Malayali workforce which would be more pliable. The labour force was recruited from the depressed classes by painting a picture of a rosy life in the hills. When these pictures turned out to be false, the contracts were enforced. By 1910, there were about eight thousand subjugated workers in the rubber plantations in around Mundakayam.

Commercial cultivation of crops by the British colonials had begun in the region in the 1870s, and at this time were also a source of employment for the educated middle class. The Syrian Christians who acquired the required skills and knowledge to manage plantations from the Europeans were in a position to acquire their own estates. They were also able to consolidate their social position as officials and members of plantation associations.

In the subsequent decades and to the present day, Syrian Christians have formed one of the largest communities to own and to work in the plantations of South India.

A NOTE ON OCCUPATIONS

Excerpted from *Madras District Gazetteers, The Nilgiris*, Volume I by W Francis, Madras (1908) p223

The weavers, dyers, cotton-cleaners, toddy-drawers, fishermen, oil-pressers, rice-pounders, lime-burners, bangle-makers, jewellers, rope-makers, metal-workers, basket-makers, leather-workers, potters and others who form so considerable a proportion of the population of the districts in the plains are extremely rare in the Nilgiris. There is, for example, perhaps not a single working weaver or dyer on the whole of the plateau.

Such industries as do exist and flourish are almost entirely those which are due to European enterprise and capital or are necessitated by the existence of Europeans in the district, and most of these have been referred to sufficiently elsewhere. They comprise the brewing at the Nilgiri and Rose and Crown breweries; the tea-factories at the Devarshola, Kodanad, Ouchterlony Valley, Liddellsdale and other estates; a few dairies, soda-water factories and printing-presses, the Cinchona Factory at Naduvattam and the Cordite Factory at Aravankad.

When the hills first became known to Europeans, enthusiasts believed that the inexhaustible supply of water-power afforded by the streams upon them would lead to the establishment there of mills and factories of every kind. But the absence (until comparatively recently) of any railway to them and the high rates of wages demanded by native labour on them were sufficient obstacles to the realization of any such dream. The ordinary native greatly dislikes life on the cold plateau away from his temples, bazaars and relations; the cost of living there, necessitating as it does warm clothing and a substantial house, is higher than on the plains; and consequently wages of all kinds rule very high. Those for unskilled labour are about double what they are in the low country.

BEARERS *from Ootacamund to Mysore or Bangalore.*

Notice is hereby given, that the Commission for the Government of Mysore having continued to Mr. Van Ingen, (the Head Clerk of the Presidency Office at Mysore,) the appointment of Agent for Bearers, all applications for posting bearers, between Karkaree and Bangalore and Kakenkotah and Bangalore, are requested to be addressed to Mr. Van Ingen, as heretofore.

Two sets of bearers will be available at each stage, and will be charged for at the following rates :

One set of Bearers and a Mussalchee.

	Rs.	A.	P.
From Bangalore to Biddedy, ...	6	0	0
" Biddedy to Chennapatam,................	6	0	0
" Chennapatam to Muddoor, ...	5	0	0
" Muddoor to Mundium, ...	5	0	0
" Mundium to Seringapatam,.............	6	0	0
" Seringapatam to Mysore, ...	5	0	0
" Mysore to Nunjengode,.................	6	0	0
" Nunjengode to Tondovady, ...	5	0	0
" Tondovady to Goondilpet,..............	5	0	0
" Goondilpet to Bundypoor, ...	5	0	0
" Bundypoor to Karkaree, ...	5	0	0
" Mysore to Chuttenhally, ...	5	0	0
" Seringapatam to Yelwall,..............	6	0	0
" Yelwall to Kenehengode,..............	5	0	0
" Kenchengode to Nunjengode,..........	5	0	0
" Mysore to Yelwall,.....................	5	0	0
" Chuttenhally to Humpapoor, ...	5	0	0
" Humpapoor to Untersuntah, ...	5	0	0
" Untersuntah to Kakenkotah, ...	5	0	0
" Kakenkotah to Bavullynalah,..........	5	0	0
For each cowry cooly per stage,....................	0	6	4

Batta will be charged per day for each set of bearers and a mussalchee at the rate of one rupee per stage, should they be obliged to wait for a traveller at their posts beyond the appointed day.

A statement of the expences, under the signature of the Agent, will be presented to travellers on their passing through Mysore ; and it is requested that payment of the bill, in *cash*, may be made to the person deputed by the Agent to receive it, and who will reside at the public bungalow at Mysore.

Travellers are advised to ascertain that bearers can be posted for them by the authorities on the Neilgherry Hills at Karkaree before they apply for bearers from Mysore to Karkaree ; or, at any rate, not to leave Goondilpet without such assurance, as the Mysore bearers will only proceed with travellers as far as Karkaree, and where they will be met by the hill bearers.

When Mysore bearers are required to be posted by travellers coming from the Neilgherry Hills at Karkaree, intimation should be sent to the Agent at Mysore, and the exact day the travellers will arrive at Karkaree must be stated, as the Mysore bearers will not remain at Karkaree during the night.

Every traveller is advised, on coming from the hills, to quit the top of the Goodaloor Ghaut early in the morning, and by this means he will reach Goondilpet, where there is an excellent bungalow and accommodation, on the same evening.

For the same reason, travellers should leave Goondilpet early in the morning, to enable the Mysore bearers to return to their stations before night-fall. This is absolutely necessary, as the bearers refuse to leave Goondilpet late in the day.

By leaving Goondilpet early in the morning, a traveller will arrive at the bungalow on the top of the Neilgherries about 6 in the evening.

Travellers by this arrangement may possibly be detained for a few hours at Goondilpet ; but, as by any other arrangement, the unfortunate bearers' lives may be sacrificed*, it is hoped that this recommendation will be duly attended to.

(Signed) C. M. LUSHINGTON,
Mysore, 17th Dec., 1831. *Commissioner.*

POPULAR AMONG THE LABOURING CLASSES

The Wynaad and The Planting Industry of Southern India, by Francis Ford, Madras (1895) p54

Employment on European plantations is popular among the labouring classes. The hours of work are comparatively short, from 7 a.m. to 4.30 p.m. at the latest, instead of from dawn to sunset as in their own villages ; and wages are paid in cash instead of in kind. Fuel is free for the gathering of it ; the water-supply is good ; medicine is dispensed to sick persons without charge, and generally the material condition of coolies on European estates is far more carefully attended to than is the case in their own villages. The great attraction of course is the facility for saving money. It is only expedient that life on a plantation should offer these advantages, otherwise there would be little inducement for men and women to

A VIEW OF THE LABOUR LINES ON CLOUDLAND DIVISION OF HIGHWAVYS ESTATE

ORIGINAL PHOTOGRAPH BY DR ARULNATHAN

leave their homes and live for three-quarters of the year in the jungle.

Mr. Srinivasa Row, a Native planter living in Mysore, speaking at the Planters' Conference held at Bangalore in 1893, remarked :- "Coolies on most estates are generally very much better treated and better housed, fed and clothed and better attended when they are sick than they expect at home in their own villages." Mr. M.N. Subbaiya, another Native planter, speaking on the same occasion on behalf of the South Mysore Native Planters' Association, said :- "There is an impression abroad that planters treat their coolies badly and use unlawful means to get them to work. We beg to say in this particular respect that it is our first duty to disabuse that portion of the public of this unfounded notion, and assure them that labourers and maistries are now the masters of the situation as it at present stands and that we are at the mercy of unscrupulous maistries and misguided coolies. We house them comfortably, get provisions for them from a considerable distance, see they are properly taken care of while sick, and in fact we do whatever we can reasonably for their comfort." Apart from the fact that the very great majority of planters are English gentlemen, brought up to regard the bully as a mean brute, no man with a grain of common-sense, having to deal with free labour, would ill-treat his coolies. To get a bad name among them would mean well-nigh ruin, for he would never be able to obtain any but the riff-raff to work for him in the future.

THE following things are, I think, necessary for the welfare of tea planting, viz.—

1st.—That all coolies should be imported for five years instead of for three years.

2nd.—That all cases of absconding or other important offence should be punished with severe flogging instead of simple imprisonment.

3rd.—That newly imported coolies should be much more strictly examined by the Civil Surgeon than they are, and those who are unfit for garden work be returned to their country, and this at the expense of the contractor who brings them up, and not at the cost of the garden.

4th.—That good roads should be made to outlying gardens in order to enable the coolies to get the benefit of a weekly bazaar. This is most important for the comfort and health of the coolies.

5th.—That Honorary Magistrates, say one planter in each district, should be appointed in order to settle any trivial case, without the expense and loss of time incurred in sending such cases to Silchar or Hylakandy courts.

If the above suggestions were carried out, it would be much for the benefit of both planter and cooly.

I think there is now every prospect of tea planting in Cachar being a success, especially if the above remarks were carried into force. In regard to my first remark, one of the greatest expenses in opening out is importing labourers; they could be imported under a five years' agreement at the same cost as for three years, and thus be a saving of two-fifths of the cost; again, a cooly, after having been three years, is just getting into his manager's method of working.

In regard to my second remark, coolies as a rule do not care for imprisonment in the least, and if flogging were introduced, it would stop a great deal of absconding and other faults. In regard to the third remark, I have had coolies sent up and passed who have never done a day's work on the garden, several cases of their having been in the same helpless state for four or five years previous to their leaving their country, and once a case of a man who had been blind from his childhood, and all these imported at a cost of from Rs. 50 to Rs. 65 per head. In regard to the fourth remark, it speaks for itself; and the fifth, that if Honorary Magistrates were appointed they should be chosen by vote, subject to the approval of the Deputy Commissioner or Protector of Labourers, and that any cooly should have the right to appeal to the Protector of Labourers; but if his appeal was not upheld, he would be subjected by him to a severer punishment than that inflicted by the Honorary Magistrate.

C. A. EGLINTON,
Manager of Dilkhosh Tea Estate, Cachar.

A LETTER FROM CA EGLINTON, MANAGER OF DILKHOSH TEA ESTATE, CACHAR, ASSAM, IN *PARLIAMENTARY PAPERS, HOUSE OF COMMONS AND COMMAND* XLVIII (48) REPORTS ON THE TEA AND TOBACCO INDUSTRIES IN INDIA, LONDON (1874) P51-52.

LIGHTNING STRIKES

Eravangalar is situated at lands' end, at the end of a 50 km hill road traversed by the local bus just once a day from Chinnamnur. After halting there for the night, the bus would start the tortuous trip back to the plains next day. From Eravangalar, the Thekkady lake is seen far below and the glinting lights of Cochin too, beyond the Sabarimala range, on clear moonlit nights. The sleepy village is tucked away in the folding hills that grow some of the finest tea in the world and is also home to about three hundred families that, like the thousands in the area, depend upon the company-owned estates for their livelihood.

Newspapers, the villagers' only window to the world, arrive only rarely; when they do, they are read loudly and exhaustively by the few who congregate at Eravangalar's only teashop. Being local leaders of the trade unions, these opinion-makers exert a tight hold over the workforce. And when they flexed their muscles, their little universe would shake.

Trade unionism has a troubled history in India. On one side stands the social divide, largely created by India's all-pervasive caste system, but also influenced, particularly in the plantations, by colonial rule. In nations with a smaller social divide, unions have been known to work peacefully with management with the common goals of higher productivity and an enlightened workforce.

In India, union leaders have historically manipulated the workforce with a vested interest. Entire industries have been destroyed by a combination of aggression and immaturity. For us, as managers of corporations, it was a challenging situation. As the face of the management, we were exposed to anger and violence from the labour unions. It was never considered that the decisions were not ours, or that we were just as dependent on the owners as the labour force was, for our own livelihood.

It was October 1981 when orders emerged from the Eravangalar tea shop for a 'lightning strike'. Jeeps with conical loudspeakers raced around the roads of the group estates participating in the strike, Highwavys, Manalaar and Venniar, blaring accusations against the management. Diwali bonus had been declared, and the demand was for double the amount though the 11.41 percent declared was well within the Bonus Act, which prescribes 8 to 20 percent of annual wages. A public meeting was held at Manalaar. Fiery speakers incited workers against the management, declaring the strike "a fight to the death".

It was impossible to predict what turn the situation would take. In Assam, where Brooke Bond owned a large group of tea estates called Doom Dooma, insurgency and political turmoil had resulted in violence. We heard reports of senior managers being kidnapped and held for ransom. Managerial staff were evacuated from Chabwa airfield with the help of the Indian Air Force.

All of a sudden, we had been thrown from placid tranquillity into a volatile, dangerous situation. Hundreds of trees were sawed down, ostensibly vandalism but very soon diverted for profit. Roads were blocked, telephone lines cut, and managers were prevented from leaving their homes. The water supply and electricity to factories and homes were disrupted. The solitary bus service to Eravangalar – its lifeline in terms of provisions and postal service – was suspended. Government departments, including Revenue, Labour and Police, were helpless as the adamant leaders pressed on. Life became miserable for the workers, who generally lived a hand-to-mouth existence, and now had no income for nearly four weeks. It was a siege-like situation for us, too. Managers of the group, Kumar Appachu, Mohammed Jamal, Ponniah and engineer Uday Kumar Samuel, came to stay with me in Manalaar bungalow. Our water supply had been cut off, and our bungalow servant Armugham tapped water from a nearby spring at night and surreptitiously brought water to the bungalow using a garden hose.

One day, having disbursed the labour wages for November, we set out in a car for a weekend break in the plains but were blocked by a mob. It was pouring with rain. We sat inside, trapped through the night, listening to shouted threats that we would be killed if we dared to try and move ahead. Tirumurthy, Deputy Superintendent of Police, deputed from the plains on special duty to ensure our safety, was so traumatised that he fell dead that night.

Many meetings were held, with attempts to negotiate by the local as well as group management, involving all estate managers and the Industrial Relations' Manager. Union leaders generally have an allegiance to a political party and follow instructions issued by the high command but in a delicate situation like this, it is invariably the personalities and capabilities of the individuals sitting around the table that decides the outcome. In this case, we had a union leader proclaiming the villainy of the management by explaining the balance sheet to the workers over a microphone. With provocative remarks he invited individuals to come up and examine it. His voice was louder than other voices that might have been able to use logic and give a closer view, which would have shown that his was a twisted and false representation of the facts. Was the management really cooking up figures and hiding their profits? The turmoil continued for twenty-one days. The jurisdictional Sub-Collector of Periyakulam camped in the estate guest house. Massive ego clashes took place between the group manager present and the trade union leader, who demonised the group manager as 'Ravana', after the villain of the epic Ramayana.

When the strike was eventually called off, it was with the bonus retained as initially declared. The workers lost wages, the management lost profits, the government lost revenues, and the country lost production. Still, the trade unions loudly proclaimed a huge victory, saying that they had forced the management to fork out an advance payment of Rs1000 to each worker, and it was to be recovered in five instalments.

The damage caused by decimating trees was eventually repaired by ever-forgiving mother nature as many younger ones flourished in the salubrious climate of Highwavys. But the thankless humans, forgetting the bitter experiences of the earlier strike, once again resorted to another protracted and equally pointless one just a few years later, another period of turbulence and violence from which much was lost and nothing gained.

THE VENERATED ELEPHANT GOD

It was August 1996, and the start of logging operations on Sirikundra. The huge eucalyptus trees planted long ago had matured and it was time to harvest them. Permission had been obtained from the forest department. The workers were poised with sharpened six-foot saws, ropes, and other tools they needed, and were ready to start. So were the mahouts with their trained elephants who stood in wait, swaying gently and flapping their ears to ward off fruit flies from around the eyes. The entire estate staff were in attendance, awaiting the arrival of the periya dorai – big boss – to perform the Ganesh Pooja. The logging, as with any other new venture, must be given an auspicious start and for this the blessings of Ganesha, the elephant-headed God, son of Shiva and Parvathi, remover of obstacles, was essential for success and prosperity.

Here, at Sirikundra, in addition to Ganesha's idol, real elephants were present too, symbolic of an authentically auspicious start to the timber operations. Yet within a month, an elephant would fall in the same place where it had been roaming free all these years. This was a huge stray tusker which had been prowling the estate and wandering into labour camps at night in search of food. Here was a case of a vegetarian animal foraging for food at night, quite an aberration of nature. Stories about this tusker include miraculous rescues as well as tragic deaths. One is the case of engineer Ravi, on transfer from Devarshola to Anamallais, driving towards the Oosimalai turning of Sirikundra Estate. It was well past midnight and his Maruti 800 was packed to the brim with his luggage and various personal effects including his television. Accompanying him were his butler, Nair, and his pet Lhasa Apso. As he turned the corner, he was suddenly faced with a massive wild tusker. The elephant began advancing, and Ravi braked hard and shot into reverse gear. The elephant advanced menacingly – and out of the dark night, a panther abruptly leapt down from the cliff above and proceeded to walk across the elephant's path, stopping it in its tracks. The rear window was obscured with luggage so Nair had to lean out to see the road behind the car and navigate Ravi's high-speed reversing. The elephant had lost momentum but charged again, and then slowed down and, seeming to lose interest, ambled away. Ravi grabbed the opportunity to race through with his cargo and passengers.

No panther intervened in the tragic case of Muniamma, the teashop owner who slept in her decrepit shed by the side of the road despite the reports and the warnings. She believed that Lord Ayyappa of Sabarimala would keep her safe always, and continued her life's routine. Sadly, one night on a rampage, the animal destroyed the teashop and killed her in the process.

With casualties rising, the ever-vigilant trade union leaders demanded instant action by the management, and rapidly escalated the matter to the authorities. The tusker was declared a 'rogue', and the Department issued orders to 'secure' the misbehaving animal. A multi-pronged attack was launched. Tractor loads of elephant grass and sugarcane for the kumkis (or trained elephants – from the Persian word kumka meaning 'to aid') and the rogue were heaped near a culvert next to the Sirikundra bungalow. Kuruba tribals walked from TopSlip elephant camp, bringing three kumki elephants for support. A veterinary surgeon brought tranquiliser shots, and forest jeeps arrived, carrying supervising officials. Everyone waited.

The tribals kept watch all night. Past midnight, the rogue appeared, trumpeted loudly and, ignoring the bait, brushed past one of the young kumkis, goring it, and took refuge inside Sirikundra bungalow. Sitting in wait with their harpoons, the sharp shooters fired. To everyone's horror, the animal slumped on all fours and rolled down the steep slope into the rivulet below, never to rise again. The dose of tranquiliser had proved fatal. The trained elephants, who were quickly brought down to prop up the slouching animal, were seen to exhibit signs of grief and shock at the ghastly event they had just witnessed.

Things had gone terribly wrong. The general procedure was that, once the elephant was safely tranquilised, the tribals would secure it by tying its legs to the nearest trees. Its vital statistics such as height, length from trunk to tail, girth; its external injuries and also the body parts like its nails, trunk and tail hairs, the targets of unscrupulous poachers, would be recorded. A revival shot would then be given into its heart. Now the elephant was dead and permission had to be obtained from the chief wildlife warden of the state to conduct a post mortem. The same veterinary surgeon conducted the post mortem, as part of which he climbed into the belly of the dead animal for relevant investigations. The carcass was subsequently cremated at the site using loads of firewood.

The post mortem had revealed that the mammoth was blind in one eye due to a bullet injury. The mystery of how this had happened was revealed to me several years later when I was General Manager for a group of plantations in Peermade and one day at a party heard an inebriated manager boast of having shot and blinded an elephant in the Anamallais, to get rid of a herd that was walking through his fields and ruining his coffee crop. This act, arising from senseless frustration, had caused an injury that had created a rogue. This in turn led to death and destruction, and eventually resulted in the killing of a noble beast who had simply roamed free on the hills that derive their name from its species.

Paravai Kavadi

Sirikundra has a Mahaliamman temple and, to signal the start of its grand festival, Thiruvizha, its large bronze bell rings out repeatedly from early in the morning. Thousands visit over the three days of various ceremonies, which culminate in the mystic ritual of Paravai Kavadi.

The ancient temple, a small but impressive structure, is built into the hill and the rear wall comprises natural rocks. Spiral steps cut into the rock lead into the sanctum sanctorum above. A small rivulet gurgling through the crevices of the rocks suddenly disappears, reappearing a few feet below to fill a tank with water, and this is seen as a miracle which makes the temple highly revered.

On festival days, loud speakers blare devotional songs, and devotees come trickling in, a crowd of pious faces, foreheads smeared with bhasmam – holy ash – and vermilion. Women in brightly-coloured finery bring trays containing flowers garlands, coconut and fruits as

Temple and festival images courtesy V Gopi, Management Assistant, Injipara

offerings to the deity. Men carrying children on their shoulders and oversized bags walk behind. The temple grounds are festooned with scalloped streamers and floral arches, and its entrance forms a large archway of fully-laden banana trees with tender coconuts hung above, to welcome the devotees. Inside, poojas are accompanied by the chanting of Vedic shlokas and ritual aartis. Fragrance exuded by the burning camphor and incense sticks combine with the scents of various flowers on offer, to fill the air with a characteristic aroma of worship.

Most of the estate workforce in the Anamallais come from the Madurai-Tirunelveli-Pollachi areas where the reigning deity is Mariamman, a form of the mother goddess who also appears as Badrakali, Durga, Parvathi, Shakti and others. Every division would have a Mariamman temple, with idols of Ganesha and Murugan – her sons. During the hot summer months, when fevers accompanied by pox viruses such as chicken pox and measles occur, it is

The Paravai Kavadi procession at Sirikundra in 1998.

believed that Mariamman is visiting the child and must be appeased. Believers make vows and commit penance. One of the most extreme forms is the Paravai Kavadi, and it was performed in Sirikundra every year.

The loud sound of the nadaswaram, accompanied by the tavil, a drum slung across the shoulder and beaten on one side with a hand and a stick on the other, herald the procession. A tractor emerges from the temple, the human Paravai Kavadi suspended in it from iron chains hooked into his back. The tractor moves slowly and the man swings in gentle motion (like a bird, a Paravai), and the crowd repeats the chant, "Muruga, Muruga!"

Several men with vels – spears – pierced through their cheeks lead the tractor, while a group of women bedecked with flowers and with shining brass pots on their heads, follow. Men and children walk along, all chanting at a higher decibel than the nadaswaram. The procession walks around the village and returns to the temple for

THE 'VEL' CAN BE SEEN THROUGH SOME DEVOTEES' CHEEKS.

the final poojas when the Paravai Kavadi is unhooked and brought down, to the continuous tolling of the bells that signal the successful completion of the ritual.

This ritual is one of extreme penance and is said to be performed by devotees who have taken a vow and observed extensive austerities and strict purification. It is believed that these men of attainment enter into a trance and do not feel any pain when their skin is pierced, testimony that absolute faith, belief and surrender to the supreme gives the mind immense control over the body.

Quite a few of them repeat the ordeal year after year, and experienced ones have a permanent hole in the skin of their backs through which the hook is suspended. These professional Paravai Kavadis, hired by the temple committee to perform their feat, collect dakshina – offerings of money – from worshippers right through the day.

A DEVOTEE IS SUSPENDED BY HOOKS INSERTED IN HIS BACK.

A MANEATER

Located in the rolling Anamallai Hills, Sirikundra is one of the oldest tea estates in the region, its name arising from the multitude of little hillocks that constitute it. Planted just before and soon after the First World War by British planters, this idyllic property enjoys salubrious climate for most of the year. Perennial rivulets run through the swamps and provide pristine water for the beautiful bungalows that dot the estate. Day follows day in this little hamlet, peaceful and tranquil. At dawn, herds of cattle come racing out of their cramped cattle sheds and are led to their grazing pastures, to return at dusk when their filled udders are harvested. Every morning, the tea-pluckers walk with baskets slung on their backs, filling them with leaves.

It seemed a day like any other. Then, as the unsuspecting women walked in single file up the hill through a narrow lane towards the field, chattering away as usual, a fullgrown Bengal tiger with outstretched paws and open claws suddenly sprang out of the bushes. With lightning speed, the beast leapt at a woman and pinned her down. Next, the tiger attacked and wounded the neighbouring plucker, who protected herself by flashing a plucking shear. The women screamed and fled.

Manager Nikhil Benegal was away that day, so the Assistant Field Officer on duty rushed to engineer M Ravi for assistance, and Ravi and his officer, Michael

Harding, drove straight to the field. Along with Field Superintendent Nandakumar and a few male workers, they made valiant efforts to chase the tiger. A male worker, Pandi, who was also skilled as a hunter, raced home and charged out with his eetti – spear. Pandi attempted to plunge it into the beast, striking its face but missing its skull, and the tiger responded by recoiling, baring its teeth and claws, and tearing into poor Pandi, who lost consciousness on the spot. When a male worker ran out with a pantham, a flame torch made of cloth rags dipped in kerosene, the tiger retreated and vanished from sight. Pandi was carried down the slope and M Ravi rushed him to hospital where he was treated by Dr Arulnathan.

The TEI team showed great spirit in facing the maneater. When attempts to tranquilise the beast failed, Nikhil ensured that a massive cage was placed at the site with a bleating goat kid inside. Twenty-four hours after its sudden appearance, the hungry animal entered the cage

and its doors were clamped shut. It was transported to Madras for rehabilitation in the Vandalur Zoo. The tigress produced cubs in captivity a few times, adding to the depleting population of tigers.

It was later learnt that this tiger had been captured and ill-treated by villagers in Vettaikaran Pudur village in the plains a few days earlier. They had managed to tranquilise it and, dumping it into the back of a Maruti Gypsy, transported it to the Grass Hills above Akkamalai Estate. The jolts and bounces of the jungle road must have injured the tiger, who was lying cramped against the metal parts of the vehicle. When its tail twitched, they stopped the Gypsy in alarm, dragged the drowsy cat out and, abandoning it on the road, speeded away. It had probably not found anything to eat for several days when it sprang out of the bushes and pounced.

Original photographs by M Ravi, engineer Unilever.
Sirikundra, 13 October 1995

AN ELEPHANT KISSED MY WINDOW

It was the night of Diwali in 1992, a day when even the whistle-stop hamlets of India reverberated with the sound of fireworks. Diehard revellers were still bursting crackers long after most on Sirikundra had gone to sleep. It was the persistent barking of our pet Lhasa Apso, Toffee, in the kitchen, that woke Rajam. Stepping out to investigate, she heard noises at the end of the long corridor that sounded like crackers in the distance. And she also heard muffled knocks on the glass-fronted front door. There, in the hazy porch light, stood a massive elephant right at our doorstep, blowing hot kisses on the glass pane. Waking me, she then rushed to the kitchen to muzzle Toffee. It is unlikely that he would be barking like this if confronted directly with an elephant, but in the safety of the closed walls he was doing so, and the fear was that the elephants might be provoked to break down doors and windows to silence him.

Looking out of the window, we could see in the brilliant moonlight that the entire lawn of the bungalow had been taken over by a herd of wild elephants. After all, it was Diwali for them too. One after the other, our solemn visitors picked up potted plants from the veranda and tossed them in the air, as we watched in helpless despair. The sporadic noise of what we had assumed were late crackers were in fact the sound of the wild herd celebrating around our home.

Finishing up with dozens of pots, the group turned to my jeep, which was parked in the porch. The biggest of the herd charged with its forehead, and pushed the hatch door to the back seat right in. The vehicle was in gear with the hand brake applied, and did not budge. A loud, frustrated trumpeting from the leader brought volunteers. Dragging, pushing and pulling, they moved the vehicle out of the porch, and in front of our eyes, systematically vandalised it. Mangled iron piping, upholstery, canvas and plastic lay strewn alongside mud, pottery and plants on the lawn and tar road.

Adding insult to injury, the police at the Aliyar Dam check post wanted proof of what had happened before they would let the jeep pass through for retrofitting. And the forest department was naturally very concerned to know whether we had harmed the elephants in any way.

THE JEEP CAN BE SEEN CONSIDERABLY DAMAGED AND PUSHED FAR FROM ITS PARKING SPOT IN THE PORCH, AND THE POTS STREWN ABOUT AND WRECKED.

As a saving grace, my employers, Tea Estates India, got a quick response from the insurance company and the jeep was returned to me as good as new in less than a week, and things were gradually restored to normal.

When we recounted the incident, people would jocularly comment on the elephants' Diwali party at our home. It dawned on us that the firecrackers and revelry must have driven the herd out of their shelters into human habitation. Deprived of fodder and water, the herd exhibited its wild frustration to us.

Since 2017, the lawns of Sirikundra bungalow, our former home, have been dotted with luxury tents, making it an envied tourist destination where people come to experience the ambience we enjoyed and took for granted for several decades. Elephants were welcome then, but today it is out of bounds for anyone who can't afford an expensive holiday!

KEEP
CALM
AND
DRINK
TEA

Serenade of the Whistling Schoolboy

The Malabar Thrush (Myophonus Horsfieldii) is a fascinating bird. Appearing black from a distance, the Whistling Schoolboy, as it is commonly called, has flashes of bright blue on its forehead and shoulders that shine brilliantly in oblique sunlight. Its melodious trilling, easy to mistake for a person whistling an unfamiliar but haunting tune, is a pleasure to listen to at dusk and at dawn, which is when they sing. Quite the opposite is the shrill screech they emit when disturbed: a harsh and daunting cry that would cause a predator to pause, giving the bird the opportunity to make good its escape.

The Malabar Thrush feeds on berries, crabs, moths, insects, earthworms and small frogs. Found singly as well as in pairs, the Whistling Schoolboy is one of the few species that haven't been threatened by human encroachment of its habitat. On the contrary, they enjoy human company, hopping around verandas, lawns and water bodies, unmindful of human presence.

The pair that used to frequent Sirikundra bungalow laid a few eggs in the nest they had built painstakingly over weeks on the wooden joint of the pillar and beam that supported the veranda. Celebrating courtship, they pranced around whistling serenades and dancing to their tunes every day. Both were ecstatic when the eggs hatched, and the pair took turns to bring baby food for the chirping young hatchlings that waited impatiently for each mouthful. Eternally rushing in or out of the nest to feed the young ones, the birds no longer had time for duets.

One evening, as Rajam and I sat and enjoyed a cup of tea, we were startled by sharp screeches from the loving pair as they flew in circles over their nest in a panic. We looked up to the ghastly sight of a huge rat snake coiled around the beam devouring the young chicks from the nest. Grabbing the nearest stick, our gardener Guruswamy chased the snake away, but by then, sadly, the chicks were all gone.

The birds were shocked by the tragedy and utterly distraught, flapping around helplessly for a while and then flying away. When they reappeared some days later, the bounce had gone, and their whistling sounded morose. They picked disinterestedly at worms and moths from the lawn.

The gap in the ceiling through which the snake had come had been sealed for good. The birds surveyed the site cautiously for weeks and when reassured, returned. Soon songs filled the air again as the whistling pair gathered nesting material from the garden. First fallen sticks and twigs, followed by dry leaves and finally feathers, to line the nest. Serenades and courtship resumed as monsoon winds heralded the commencement of rains.

It wasn't long before the chirping of the new born chicks could be heard once again from the security of their warm and cosy nest.

SPORT IS EXCELLENT

Excerpted from *The Wynaad and The Planting Industry of Southern India*, by Francis Ford, Madras (1895) p20

Sport in the Wynaad is excellent. Bungalows lie two or three miles apart ; there is no population except the people who live in the occasional villages and small towns, the indigenous forest tribes who sparsely inhabit the district and a few cultivators residing on the edges of the swamps. All kinds of big game abound, but as there is plenty of cover and it is seldom possible to beat, the man who makes good bags much be a student of woodcraft. Luck of course at times favours. Here are one or two recent instances. A planter was strolling round his estate early in the evening, a gun over his arm, his dogs with him. As he rounded a corner, on the same path as he was walking not twenty yards off stood a sambhur stag, an antlered monarch. The gun was loaded with shot ; he unloaded, pushed in a ball cartridge and fired. A clean miss ; the stag galloped off, then halted, giving time for another cartridge to be put in. The aim was better and the beast brought to book. On a plantation, near a Government reserve forest, the owner having set his coolies to work, strolled into the jungle in the hope of coming on bison. He was following up their tracks when he was suddenly confronted by two elephants. As they were heading for him, he fired, and as they swerved, gave one his second barrel, hitting it through the heart and rolling it over like a rabbit. To bag an elephant casually before breakfast does not happen every day. This same planter has shot sambhur from his verandah ; he has slain bear and panther between tea and dinner, without beating or doing more than walking or waiting quietly on the hillside, not a mile from the house. His bungalow is one of the best-known in the Wynaad and it is not considered either particularly isolated or buried in the jungle. Another planter, who lived but a quarter of a mile from the main district road and within a furlong of a small town, was walking down his carriage drive one evening. The coffee lay below him and on a big rock, not forty yards off, a tiger lay sunning itself. However his luck was out, for though he had time to go back to the house and get a rifle, the first cartridge missed fire, and before he was able to put in the other (the rifle was single barreled), the big beast had discovered the danger and disappeared. These stories read like romances, but they are the absolute truth and nothing but the truth ; and many more similar ones could be told. It is not the slightest exaggeration to say that big game is as common in the Wynaad as hares and partridges in an English county, but as a man may walk miles at home without seeing either, so in the Wynaad, with its thick and abundant cover, he may go days without being confronted by a monarch of glen or jungle; moreover in the latter country there are infinitely greater difficulties in coming up with quarry than in England.

CHOICE MORSELS

Excerpted from *The Nilgiri Guide and Directory* by JSC Eagan, Madras, (1916) p142

The Rib-Faced or Barking Deer, commonly known as the jungle sheep, is found all over the Hills, and affords some sport.

THE DEER THAT ATE UP ALL OUR ROSES

One of the most beautiful species of the deer family is the Muntjac, commonly called the barking deer. In India, this small deer can be seen right from the Himalayan ranges to the lowest slopes of the Western Ghats. Its brilliant brown coat, cautious, tentative walk, short sweptback antlers and the loud shrill barks that waken the jungle have all made this the most endeared member of the deer family. The swift-footed barking deer can flee at lightning speed at the first sign of threat. At dawn and dusk, barking deer families would visit our

ORIGINAL PHOTOGRAPH OF BARKING DEER BY RUDRAKSHA CHODANKAR

bungalow and graze in the garden for the fresh fruit and vegetables that it offered them round the year. On some moonlit nights we could see them, young and old, tiptoe stealthily onto the lawn and nibble at the tender shoots of grass, always alert, sniffing the air for danger signals at intervals, settling back when reassured, or rapidly straightening to flee. In the morning, the place would be littered with deer droppings and fresh hoof marks on the dew-covered lawn.

One year, during the summer showers, we pruned about a hundred rosebushes that lined our large lawn. The regrowth flourished and in a few months, dozens of flower buds appeared in each one of the bushes, such a glorious sight! But one night a family of barking deer entered the garden to graze and we woke to see that every one of the roses, buds and all, were gone. Enraged, we instructed the gardener to lay a trap and catch the deer. And sure enough, next morning we woke to the news that a full-grown male barking deer had been captured. Uneasy, we sat down to breakfast with the unspoken thought, "Oh no! What are we going to do now?" Arjun and Nandita, seven and four at the time, inquired with concern why there was a deer tied up behind the bungalow. Wouldn't it be hungry and thirsty? Shouldn't we feed it? We explained that animals don't readily eat in captivity, at which they insisted that the deer be untied and set free. Of course this was the right solution. We released the creature, and it darted off into the dense thicket below.

THE OOTACAMUND HUNT

Nilgiri Guide and Directory, A handbook of general information upon the Nilgiris for visitors and residents by JSC Eagan. Madras 1916 p39

Nowhere, 'east of Suez,' is there so grand a field for the sport, nor in the Motherland itself is fox-hunting so keenly pursued, as on the Nilgiris, with the Ootacamund Hunt. From a very humble beginning, the Club now has a reputation which is almost as well known at Home, as it is throughout India. Brooksby, in The Field, writing of hunting on these Hills, says :- 'This is a wild, sporting country in which English fox-hounds are not wanted, where game is plentiful, and the problem of scent is (locally) solved.' Again, 'Oh, worshipful Master of England, this country has its advantages after all. No riding over hounds when they are running here, no scuttling forward and cutting off the track as they turn under a hedgerow. Not the wisest citizen that ever migrated to Milton, to stick one more thorn into the already lacerated sides of Firr or Gillard could work much mischief here. There is always a scent, and as the hounds must often start close at their game, it is all that the stoutest of waler blood, sent along by the keenest and youngest of spurs, can do to live with them.'

The history of the sport in Ooty dates back as far as 1845, when Lieut. (afterwards Sir) Thomas Peyton started the first regular pack, though fox hounds were introduced on the Nilgiris as far back as 1829 ; but were used for beating the sholas for game, and later hunted the elk or sambhur. After a very precarious career in the interval, the Hunt Club, as it exists today was thoroughly organized and regularly started, by Mr. J. W. Breeks, the first Commissioner of the Nilgiris in 1869. During the last twenty years the Hunt has become established on a larger and firmer basis, and in most respects equals the ordinary provincial pack in England.

In 1896, Lord Wenlock, then Governor of Madras, was instrumental in reserving thirty square miles of grass and shola to the west of Ooty which is now known as the 'Wenlock Downs.'

The hunting country lies to the west of Ootacamund and consists of rolling downs, interspersed with streams and bogs and hills of considerable altitude. There is practically no jumping. The banks of the streams are generally rotten owing to rats ; otherwise, the going is sound and good, and chiefly of grass. The swamps can only be crossed by the special crossings constructed by the hunt. Hounds run extremely fast with no hedges to impede them, and it takes a good horse and a good rider to live with them. An eye for country is a valuable asset to the new-comer.

The Hill Jackal is a fine animal, and unless severely pursued at the start can hold its own with the fastest hounds and beat them.

THE MAGNIFICENT OOTACAMUND CLUB, HISTORICAL SITE WHERE SNOOKER WAS FIRST PLAYED. OOTY 1985. FROM SAAZ'S ALBUM.

HOW TO CATCH A SNAKE

Vandiperiyar and Peermade are contiguous hill ranges situated in the Kerala section of the Western Ghats, at altitudes of about 3000 feet above the sea level. Once the retreat of the maharajas of Travancore, the ruins of two of their summer palaces form a point of interest for tourists today. These hills are replete with plantation crops like coffee, tea and rubber, and spices, such as pepper, cardamom, clove and cinnamon. Abundant with fruit trees and cash crops, these ranges are among the richest in South India.

Being spread out over a fairly large area, life on the estates was lonely and the British pioneers built clubs where planters could play sports and enjoy each other's company. The Vandiperiyar Club invited membership from planters of its roughly thirty estates. Besides a bar and pantry, and facilities for tennis, billiards, table tennis and bridge, the club also had one of the best libraries in the district with an extensive collection of books, mostly donated by expatriates leaving to return 'home'. The club also subscribed to popular magazines; in the early days it was *Good Housekeeping*, *Women's Weekly* and others, and later Indian news and feature publications. Peermade, about 15 kilometres from Vandiperiyar, also had a well-equipped club, and in addition to the features of Vandiperiyar, also had a nine-hole golf course. The two clubs combined during big planting events and hosted large sports competitions for other districts in the region.

It so happened that one evening Sunil and Vinu Sivaraman, friends of ours who lived on a neighbouring estate, were returning home from a visit to the club library in their open jeep and had to step out into a gentle drizzle to raise the barrier at an unmanned estate check post. The ground and trees were damp. When the bamboo pole was lifted to let the car through, the pole probably touched tree branches overhead as Vinu felt a blob of water fall on her lap.

Back in the comfort of their home, Vinu left the books that had lain in her lap on a sofa. After dinner, she sat next to the pile and looked through them to pick something to read when a green, slimy creature slithered over her hand, dropped onto the carpet and glided out of the French windows into the garden. It was a shock – but, because of their relatively lower altitude, these hills are sanctuaries for a variety of reptiles, and encounters with snakes are quite common. We were not surprised to hear this story.

While snakebite is invariably lethal in the plains, the snakes that inhabit higher altitude are less poisonous. The dangers include festering snakebite, and treatment with a medicine that reacts with the poison and can cause harm.

The very next week, stepping into the pantry after an evening stroll, I saw in the dim light a movement under my outstretched legs. Stunned at the sight of a dark brown snake, I froze in horror and then withdrew my legs very carefully, and slipped out to the porch to send for Sundar.

Those days I was Group Manager of Hope Plantations

and living on Glenmary, one of the many tea estates in India with Scottish names bestowed by nostalgic planters of yore seeking to transport a sense of their beloved Highlands to the western ghats. When Sundar eventually sauntered in half an hour later, he was roaring drunk.

Sundar was a worker on the estate, a pruner. However, he had an additional duty, for which he was sometimes in much demand. Somehow, when he arrived, he knew exactly where to look for the snake, finding it without any hesitation or ceremony or false moves in a massive rosewood root that lay in the corner, a beautiful piece we had carried home as a decoration. Skilfully employing the fork at the end of the long stick which he always carried about with him, in one easy move Sundar displayed his booty: a pit viper with a triangular head and markings all over its body.

It's impossible to know how Sundar could sense where to find the snake. Perhaps he could smell it. There's no doubt that the poor creature knew it was being hunted and would be hiding to protect itself, and he had a good idea about snake hiding places. Once he was on the scene, and no matter how inebriated he was – in fact, the more

A SNAKE CHARMER, MYSORE, 1966
ORIGINAL PHOTOGRAPH BY CAROLYN HOLLIS

the better is the reputation he had – he would go straight to the spot and in a flash the snake would be dangling at the end of his stick. Sundar would then hold it down and display his prowess by showing whether it was a male or female specimen. He would demonstrate his lack of fear as well as his superior knowledge of the creature by pointing out its poison glands and report on how much poison they contained, what variety, and how much damage it could do.

It's not clear why alcohol was such a vital part of Sundar's snake-catching process! Perhaps it was to pump him with courage, or perhaps it was a time to celebrate, or perhaps it helped open up a third eye he needed for the job. After all, snakes have always been a vital part of Hindu mythology, being the creature that Lord Shiva wears around his neck like a garland. Snake carvings and statues find pride of place in Shiva temples, sometimes phalanxes of them. There are myths of snakes who wait to strike and kill in revenge for the loss of a mate, and there are places where worshippers leave eggs, milk, bananas and other offerings near a snake hole or Sarpa Kavu temple open to the sky, and the creatures are seen to consume them and then lie nearby, sunning their coils. And, with the phallic connotations of a snake, Naga Puja is sincerely believed to cure childlessness. Snakes were an important element of worship on the estates and most of our temples had shrines. And so, the snakes that were caught were generally not eaten or harmed in any way. After Sundar had completed his performance, he would walk with the snake to the edge of the estate and, lowering it from his stick, would release it into the wild.

the symbol of business efficiency

Carbon Papers

Hands, copies and desk remain
clean when Kores carbon paper
is used. The copies are sharp,
legible and difficult to smudge.
Kores carbon papers are very
economical on account of their
durability.

Typewriter Ribbons

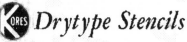

It is a pleasure to type with a
Kores ribbon. The impressions
are well defined and positive
from the very first day. Kores
ribbons will not smudge even
when new and each ribbon
gives 20 lakhs impressions.

Drytype Stencils

With Kores Drytype Stencils
the types of the typewriter
remain clean and do not fill up.
Round letters do not fall out
and the typewriter rollers remain unaffected. Kores Drytype Stencils are also ideal for
drawing and hand work.

Kores (India) Limited manufacture Carbon Papers, Type-
writer Ribbons, Drytype Duplicating Stencils, Duplicating
Ink and Accessories, Ink Tablets, Stamp Pads and Stamp
Pad Inks.

KORES PRODUCTS are obtainable from all stationers

KORES (INDIA) PRIVATE LTD.   Bombay - Madras - Delhi - Calcutta

REPRODUCED FROM *PLANTING DIRECTORY OF SOUTHERN INDIA*, COMPILED BY

THE SECRETARY, UPASI, COONOOR (1956)

Life among the cows

A sweet memory contributed by Nandita Ravindran

With us growing children in the family, we always had a milking cow and its calf in the bungalow cattle shed. They were either Jersey or Holstein Friesian breeds. On the estates, the birth of a calf was often celebrated with sweets being distributed, though if the calf was male, one had to make do with boiled toffee. The high yielding cow Paapatti (or Goddess) of Injipara was very docile, and even let the children play with her calf. Gurang would also join the fun at times. Daisy at Sirikundra, on the other hand, was not so friendly, being particularly protective of her calf and very suspicious of two-wheelers.

It was year 1999, just the beginning of the internet era in India, and the estate management had installed a computer with dial-up internet connectivity which worked for about an hour every afternoon. Emails were the latest mode of communications and I was visiting from college for my annual summer vacation. Every afternoon I visited the office to send and receive emails from my friends.

One day, as I was returning to the bungalow, riding an old worn-out and very slow moped, it happened that Daisy was grazing nearby. Daisy had recently delivered a calf which was in the cattle shed at the back of the bungalow. The moment Daisy saw my strange moped making its peculiar guttural noises, her urge to protect her little one kicked in, and she started chasing me. I was not expecting this kind of attack, and was caught unawares and suddenly found myself fleeing up the kind of very steep hill on which most plantation bungalows are located, on a vehicle that could not move faster than 30kmph. My frantic revving of the bike further infuriated Daisy, who raced forward with her tail hoisted high, snorting and mooing loudly.

It so happened that my grandfather was visiting us at this time, and was taking a stroll on the sprawling lawns, plodding along with his walking stick. On

NANDITA WITH CAT MOKSHU, DAISY'S CALF AND DOG TOFFEE

seeing Daisy charging behind me, he felt responsible for defending his granddaughter and set off, charging behind Daisy with his stick raised high in the air screaming "Eh, eh, eh!"

I finally reached the end of the path, which was the car shed, with Daisy in hot pursuit barely inches away. Dropping the moped on the ground, I leapt onto the white Ambassador car standing in the garage, and clambered to the top.

Daisy reached the fallen moped, sniffed at it, and realised that it was not much danger to her calf. My grandfather was able to shoo Daisy away. Hearing and seeing the spectacle, all the bungalow staff came running to the spot and, once it was clear that no damage had been done, everyone collapsed in splits of laughter and Daisy resumed her grazing where she had left off.

Bees in the attic

DENIS AT 23, IN INDIA

Denis Mayne reports from Belfast

My bungalow on Prospect was run by Thomas the cook and butler Sussie. Between them they managed to produce some tasty if rather solid meals. They insisted on serving a three-course lunch every day which I found daunting, but when I tried to persuade them to provide a lighter meal they shuffled their feet and assumed such hang-dog expressions that I was moved to let the matter rest. I continued to eat three-course lunches followed by a short convalescent snooze.

When I was invited to meals in the homes of Indians, I noticed that all the food was placed on the table at the start and the diners dipped into dishes of their choice. I assumed that this was the reason why Sussie never quite sorted out the order in which courses were served. One day it was main course, soup and pudding, another day it was pudding, soup and main course until all possible permutations had been covered, but not necessarily in a regular sequence.

Although the standard of food was good, I became aware of a steady rise in the quality of the puddings, no matter where they arrived in the order of service. It transpired that Thomas had been having cooking lessons from Ramesh, my neighbour Peter Sausman's butler. Ramesh was one of those people who can only be described as a Superior Being. Tall and slim in his white tailored butler's livery, he carried an air of refined expectation of all things being proper and in his presence I felt a need to be on best behaviour. He also had the spooky gift of appearing about three seconds before he was called. Among his many excellent qualities was his culinary expertise, a talent which he had acquired at his first employment where the doraisani had taught him a number of English recipes. This was unusual, for most doraisanis were dreadful cooks, producing fierce 'curries' that bore little resemblance to any genuine Indian dish.

Ramesh was particularly proud of his repertoire of cakes and puddings and would recite them enthusiastically. This was an entertaining experience for, while he had an excellent command of English, he had his own idiosyncratic pronunciation. For instance, he called a cake a "kack" which is a word shared by Hindi and Gaelic, but does not mean cake in either. If required he could produce "Chocolate Kack", "Victory Spongey Kack", "Mydeary Kack" and one of his own favourites, "Chocolate Hitlers" which translated as chocolate éclairs. But my choice above all others was his superb "Queenie Pudding" where the fluffy meringue and the lightly-set custard with a thin layer of jam between were combined to perfection.

It was while enjoying a Queenie Pudding that I was surprised by a soft thump on the ceiling followed by a low buzzing sound. Unperturbed I continued with my pudding until Sussie burst into the room pointing excitedly at a corner of the ceiling where a thin cord of bees was emerging from a very small hole. He urged me to leave the room at once. But I was enjoying my pudding too well to allow a few bees to distract me. Determined not to waste a crumb I slid the spoon round the empty plate for one last time and stood up to find I was surrounded by a galaxy of swirling bees. Sussie was almost apoplectic by now as I walked from the room in a controlled and, I hoped, dignified fashion, leaving the majority of the bees in the room.

A crowd had gathered to view the dorai eating his lunch in a beehive. It is a feature of Indian life that any unusual incident attracts an instant audience. The local bee-man had been called, a profoundly deaf hermit who lived in the jungle communicating with his bees and bartering their honey for a living. Upon his arrival the spectators parted with reverent respect. He climbed confidently through a trap door into the roof space and reappeared barely a minute later. He dropped nimbly to the floor accompanied by a cloud of excited bees causing us to draw back to give them space as they passed. The man, now clothed with bees, walked with the concentrated dignity of a priest performing a ritual, his outstretched arms bearing a small box like a miniature ark of the covenant. His passage from the bungalow was marked by a bush of bees moving above the tea and we continued to watch as the swarm glided past the workers lines, along a path by the stream before vanishing through a gap into the jungle.

Never bathe in a thunderstorm

The Prospect bungalow bath was constructed of white floor-tiles that made it look like a municipal bath. It was wide and very deep so when I was sitting in it the water came up to my shoulders. The joints between the tiles were not smooth and scratched as I slid up and down. Every evening upon my return from the field, hot water boiled in a petrol barrel over an open log fire at the rear of the kitchen, was carried to the bath in kerosene oil cans. Cold water travelled to the bath tap through a metal pipe laid over-ground from a tank near the top of the hill behind the bungalow. Once all the hot water was in the bath, I mixed it with cold until the

Denis at 80, with his wife Anne in their garden in Ireland.

temperate reached a comfortable level when I could luxuriate with just my head protruding above the water. After a day in the field it was a pleasingly sensual experience. One evening, however, I was rudely jolted from my reveries. I had just soaped myself and was nonchalantly twiddling the tap with my toes when suddenly there was a brilliant flash of lightning accompanied by a fearfully loud clap of thunder. In an instant I discovered myself covered in soap standing beside the bath with the water still sizzling. The lightning had scored a bull's eye on the water pipe.

I was in India from 1961 to 1964. It was a fantastic experience and I loved the country, its history and culture. My biggest learning was to discover that we are all people. The workers were very poor, the older ones were completely illiterate, but they were no different from me except that I had a bigger house, servants, smart clothes and the advantage of education. They had all the emotions I felt, and also an extraordinary ability to debate and argue. They influenced me for the rest of my life to enjoy and appreciate the company of anybody. But I had a big row with my manager, Bonzo Atkinson, which made me think about my future in India. I was disappointed by the apparent continued separation of the Indian and European communities. In the end I felt like an interloper. There was still too much of the atmosphere of British superiority, too much deference shown to me even by well-educated Indians. I returned to Belfast to run my family's bookstore.

BUTLERS OF PLANTATION BUNGALOWS

When the British finally departed, they left behind not only a vast network of railways connecting the Indian hinterland, postal service, bridges and so on, but also a valuable resource called the butler.

Originating from the biblical book of Genesis, Wikipedia tells me that 'butler' is a derivative of the Anglo-Norman 'butelier', corresponding to old French 'botellier', which means officer-in-charge of the king's wine bottles ('bouteille' being French for bottle). The butler's role clearly had to do a lot with caring for and serving wine and other bottled beverages, and quite a few of the native butlers in British service took this part of their job very seriously.

Once, nearly fifty years ago, officers at the Staff College in Wellington decided to fix the butler, who was suspected to be habitually pinching from a bottle of French Brandy. The level of alcohol was found to be consistently diminishing from their precious military quota.

The officers were determined to catch the culprit. One day, after several shots of booze, they conceived a brilliant idea and, snorting with laughter, filled up an empty brandy bottle with fresh urine, and slipped it into the bar. Seeing the level in the new bottle gradually declining, the officers would be in splits. Their get-togethers became louder each day with roars of laughter, until when the bottle was nearly empty, they summoned the culprit –

and were stricken to hear the mortified butler, trembling with fear, confess that he had been adding liberal doses from the new bottle to the puddings he made for the officers every day.

Closer to home, I was having a drink with a friend one evening and saw him grimace after the first sip. The matter of his rum having been watered down was a solemn one indeed and he took it up straight away with my butler who indignantly defended himself by saying that he had been very highly regarded in British times (the insinuation being that we were only finding fault with him because, being natives, we weren't good enough for him). Clearly the time had come for me to inspect the liquor cabinet and I felt shocked and betrayed to see precious bottles, which I had been saving for important occasions, cloudy with algae that had grown

SUBBU BUTLER STANDS IN THE PORCH OF THE WOODBROOK
BUNGALOW TO WELCOME A VISITOR'S CAR.
IMAGE COURTESY VICTOR & JINI DEY

out of the water my Jeeves had been topping them up with! Interestingly, the bottles of local brew had all been left intact for the master. Clearly, the masters might admonish their "Jeeves" for his lapses, but the butlers too were viewing their bosses with disdain as some of them could hardly tell Crème de Menthe from Drambuie or Yorkshire pudding from Christmas pudding!

The plight of the butler in those days was a poignant one indeed. With the colonial masters gone, the rug had been pulled out from under their feet, but they were still expected to manage huge plantation bungalows with retinues of servants, . Donning the previous master's woollen suit and shoes, the butlers did an efficient job of serving the new Indian masters under the democratic setup. But there were times when it was they who made the decisions. I remember my early days on the plantations when I was still craving the idli breakfast I was accustomed to. Butler Lakshman was appalled that I was turning down his standard eggs-and-toast. He had heard of idlis, in fact he had even eaten them (very rarely and a very long time ago no doubt) but he had no idea how they were made. I remained firm in my demand, and poor Lakshman went away to embark on the required research. A few days later, with trembling hands, he presented me with the budget, which read:

1. Mash making stone.

2. Loading Cooli.

3 Unloading Coolie.

4. Idlie making vessel.

5. Rice.

6. Black dhall.

The stove at Prospect in 1998, long past its days of glory baking
fish for Sir John, no longer used at all.

The stoves in the old estate bungalows used firewood as a fuel that
also heated a boiler right behind the stove, which was usually in
a separate room or shed. When it was at an elevation, hot water
could be piped to the bathtubs and wash basins in the bungalow.
In some bungalows, the hot room, heated by the boiler, was very
useful to dry clothes. Pets found it a haven in extra-cold weather!

FROM SAAZ'S ALBUM.

The cost of these items amounted to Rs107, nearly half my monthly salary. I had to forego my longing for idli.

Gradually, estate kitchens that once served bacon and sausages gave in to dosais and puris. The wood-fired cast iron ovens that once produced tarts and pies now smouldered grudgingly, often used for nothing more than drying firewood. Grinding dough became a daily chore. Steaks and soups submitted to pulao and sambar. Smoked salmon, rare steak, roast pork and turkey with stuffing, bywords of our time, became nostalgic memories.

In his previous avatar, a butler might be assigned to bring cases of scotch whiskey, riding on the master's stallion from ports afar. He would accompany them on a duck shoot or a game hunt. In pouring rain, he might be assigned to don his master's shoes, rain coat and helmet and ride around the fields, not only to deceive his master's boss but also to ensure that workmen did not malinger during the downpour. He would work desperately hard in succession planning, to train the cusni-matey in his skills. It was a difficult job and stories abound of the trainees bringing shoes for their masters in tea-trays with quivering hands, and of serving them cold fried eggs which had been stored in the refrigerator.

That era passed, long ago, and today many of the old plantation bungalows have been converted to holiday homes – business ventures catering to affluent holiday seekers. The morphed butler of today is a successful hospitality professional, bringing to his clients the excellent service that we once enjoyed as part of our lives and took so much for granted.

PLASTIC WAS ONCE GREETED WITH JOY

The day my appointment letter arrived, I grabbed a pen to sign it but my mother stopped me. "Wait," she said, "Don't use that! Sign with the pen your father presented you." After all, it was August 1967 and this was my first job. I pulled out the precious black Swan pen with a gold clip and a golden nib, and did so. I remember a few more such gifts, relics from a loving father – one was a Dunlop tennis racquet autographed by the then Wimbledon champion, Lew Hoad. Another was a suit-length from the sought-after Indurex of England: "By appointment to Her Majesty, the Queen of England," a red ribbon attached to the fabric with a wax seal specified. Suit-making was a superior skill had by only a few. In Madras there was one Syed Bawker, who was known to have tailored suits for matinee idol Shivaji Ganesan, and that's where we got my suit made.

Once my appointment was confirmed and I was preparing to leave home for the first time to join the plantations, my father took me to Poppat Jamal's in Parry's Corner, Madras, to kit me out. It was 1967. He bought me a full porcelain 34-piece dinner set comprising plates, quarter-plates, soup bowls, soup spoons, pudding bowls, serving plates and serving dishes; a cutlery set, kitchen utensils, bed and bath linen, and everything I needed to start a new home. My umbrella was made of thick canvas and had a wooden handle. I had a fully-rubberised Duckback raincoat, and my coat hangers and clothes pegs were wooden. All this was packed into a huge aluminium chest of the type used by captains of ships. Over time, the heavy iron trunks that were used on long journeys were replaced by leather-covered cardboard suitcases.

In my early years in the Nilgiris, tea-pluckers carried reed baskets on their backs to collect harvested leaves. Two baskets were issued per head per year. They were also issued field cumblies – woollen blankets, made of 'shoddy', an inferior variety of lamb's wool, which was made stiff with starch derived by grinding seeds of tamarind and pressing them flat with hot coals. These were worn over their heads to protect them from the weather. Children in crèches rocked on wooden horses and played with wooden toys, as yet unpainted with poisonous lead paint. Buckets were made of iron or aluminium; ropes were of coir or hemp. Roofs of buildings were corrugated sheets of galvanized iron, or terracotta or slate tiles over wooden rafters. Doors and windows were wooden; floors and walls were plastered in cement. Water tanks were built with granite or bricks and concreted using cement.

When plastic gradually entered this world in the mid-1970s, it was a revolution that transformed our lives in a very positive way. In the tea nurseries, polythene

REGISTERED TRADE MARK
MADURACO

SALT-GLAZED
STONEWARE PIPES

Conforming to the British Standard Specifications as regards dimension, absorption and hydraulic tests, these stoneware pipes are widely used for irrigation, water supply and drainage purposes by the Govt., Railways and big estates. These are available in 4", 6", 9" and 12" dia. with spigot and socket ends and necessary specials, viz. Bends, Tees, Ys, Gully Traps etc. You can use these low porosity pipes safely for sewers and corrosive liquids. Against definite orders, unglazed Terracotta Pipes used for land drains, water conduits, septic tanks, dispersals etc. can be manufactured.

Manufactured by:
FEROKE TILE WORKS
FEROKE   S. INDIA
Proprietors:
MADURA CO. PRIVATE LTD., P.B. No. 45, KOZHIKODE-I.

FROM *PLANTING DIRECTORY OF SOUTHERN INDIA*, UPASI, COONOOR
(1956)

sleeves were introduced as a convenient means to plant vegetative cuttings of clones. Unlike in the terracotta pots used earlier, the extent of root growth could be seen through the transparent thick-gauge polythene sleeve, which was open at both ends to prevent water logging: each season, every estate would use hundreds of thousands of them. In the fields, plastic hoods replaced the cumblies and were far more effective in keeping people dry, a boon indeed for the labour whose cumblies would never be completely dry in the rainy season.

The heavy brass spraying machines were replaced by lightweight motorised power sprayers or hand-operated knapsack sprayers. The coir leaf bags once used to transport green leaf to factories were replaced by lightweight plastic-knitted green leaf bags. The jute gunny sacks that carried massive loads of fertiliser were replaced by polypropylene and high-density polyethylene woven sacks. Very soon from furniture to tarpaulins to packaging liners to floor tiles – synthetic materials replaced natural ones. Plumbing pipes, previously made of galvanized iron, and sewage pipes previously made of glazed earthen ware or cast iron, were both replaced by PVC pipes. Along with the blessing of pure drinking water – in a country where failure to boil water sufficiently long before cooling and drinking it meant the risk of jaundice, typhoid and cholera – came the plastic bottle in which it was packaged. The dreaded glass syringes with their thick needles used for our annual vaccinations against these illnesses were replaced by disposable plastic syringes with thin needles which were less painful.

Technology was bringing a parallel revolution in the fields too. In the 1970s, chemical weedicides followed by the introduction of Gramoxone, a powerful herbicide, made the manual operations on the plantations less intensive. This led to savings in manual labour and supervision and much larger areas could be kept free of weeds in less time. Since the fertile top soil was no longer ruffled by weeding, it reduced soil erosion in the heavy monsoon. Very soon the market was flooded with stronger weedicides and pesticides which naturally led to indiscriminate use. A time would come when the ill-effects outweighed the benefits.

Many of the new plastic products too had operational benefits and facilitated easier working. However, by the 1990s, a rapid dilution of quality became evident. A time came when all our chemical and paint containers, water cans and bottles were made of plastic. Royal Doulton cisterns in the toilets were replaced with locally-made plastic ones. Gleaming rosewood toilet seats gave way to inferior plastic replacements. Plastic bags indiscriminately replaced the equally useful paper and cloth bags previously used.

Looking back, it is clear that the speed of transformation was such that the danger of plastic and chemicals to the environment became apparent only after too much irreversible damage had taken place. By then, however, our world had changed too – it had ceased to be the gracious place of elegant lifestyles and impeccable values that it had once been.

THE WEDDING GIFT

One of my amusing recollections is the classic replacement of a high-value metal with a plastic curio, in the case of Kunjappa the contractor, in the early 1970s.

Kunjappa was a minor building contractor, who could be relied on to carry out certain tasks required on the estate, such as providing workmen to lop down shade trees, supply firewood and so on. The day came when Kunjappa was invited to the grand wedding of the estate's manager in his home town and he cast about for ideas on what sort of gift he should carry for the important occasion. The boss was firm: he would not dream of accepting a big gift from any estate vendor. However, when he agreed to accept a 'small' gift, there was a faraway look of anticipation in his eyes as he rotated the 'small' golden ring on his finger.

Kunjappa was fated to disappoint his dorai – boss – in more ways than one. He arrived at the wedding, where a line of guests was walking up to greet the new couple, discreetly slipping small boxes or gift envelopes containing cash or cheques into their hands. Kunjappa carried a large, prominent gift-wrapped box and thrust it on his embarrassed manager. More embarrassment was in wait when he later unwrapped the gift in the presence of his friends and colleagues. It was a two-foot plastic coconut tree with a toddy tapper sitting on top to tap fresh toddy, while his bare-breasted wife stood below, holding a vessel ready for the brew.

The planter, disgusted with what he thought was a silly and inappropriate gift, discarded it before returning to the estate. So, on Kunjappa's next visit, he was disappointed to find that it was not on display in the boss's home. After all, he had put a lot of thought into it and found something unique and symbolic, something he found truly beautiful, and had expected that it would be given pride of place amidst the carved rosewood Edwardian furniture, Mirzapur carpets, and other vintage fittings in the bungalow. When he asked, the dorai explained without missing a beat that his mother had liked the gift very much so he had given it to her. The sincere and affectionate contractor left, only to return the next day with an exact replica of the coconut tree and, beaming all the while, placed it on the centre table of the drawing room, before taking leave of his dazed boss.

Another time in the 1980s, an affluent colleague celebrated his son's wedding in Hyderabad. It was a lavish and colourful affair, attended by the glitterati of Hyderabad. Quite a few of us from the estates attended too. We were there when our favourite trade union leader, Murugiah, walked in with his invariable retinue of followers, carrying an enormous horizontal object wrapped in newsprint and tightly bound with jute twine.

Climbing onto the grand stage to greet the new couple, he took hold of the microphone and, in the course of his address, peeled off the newspaper wrapping and proudly displayed his wedding gift. The guests were bemused to see a large plastic German shepherd with rolling eyes, menacing teeth and bright pink jaws and protruding tongue. He concluded by explaining that, "a fierce and frowning boss must be given a befitting gift!" and left with a flourish.

After all, it was a time when the world was a far simpler place, and moulded plastic was still a precious novelty!

REPRODUCED FROM *PLANTING DIRECTORY OF SOUTHERN INDIA*, COMPILED BY THE SECRETARY, UPASI, COONOOR (1956)

CARRINGTON, THE JAIL THOTTAM

Thiashola is a special place, located at close to 7000 feet, and famous for the high quality tea it produces. In 1995, I was transferred here to be trained in the art of orthodox manufacture. For more than twenty years, from the time I had worked with NSV Sinniah to set up CTC manufacture at Seaforth, that had been my domain. My employer, Tea Estates India, were now grooming me to head the manufacturing function of the company.

Out on an inspection a few days after I joined, I walked between Thiashola Division and Carrington Division with my field officer BB Raman, a member of the Badaga tribe indigenous to the Nilgiris, and I noticed the ruins of an old building covered in undergrowth. Remnants of mud walls were visible, and parts of a roof which had collapsed lay in a decrepit heap on the side. Raman told me that this was the old Carrington Jail. He was quite knowledgeable about the building and pointed out the walls demarcating the few rooms, explaining that there were no separate cells, but a couple of large dormitories in which prisoners would have huddled in the cold. Besides a small room for the jail superintendent, there were two other rooms which appeared to have an administrative function, and there was an annex at the side.

Raman explained that the Carrington Jail had been built to house Chinese prisoners of the British, who were brought from Mettupalayam through the Kundah valley to be housed here. It was believed, he said, that when Thiashola Estate was established in 1859, it was the Chinese prisoners who planted tea that gave Carrington the sobriquet "Jail Thottam" – jail garden. And garden it was indeed, with unbroken sheets of small-leaved China tea growing on undulating hills in biting cold, under a thick shade of silver oak and acacia that protected it from wind and frost. Blossoms of spathodia, jacaranda and rhododendron added their beauty to the beautiful garden. Climbing rose-trailed pergolas led into bowers that were interspersed in the three lawns of the bungalow. "Picture perfect," wrote Mr MG Raghava Menon, the company's first Indian chairman, in his visit reports of Thiashola, a glowing tribute to the fine management of the garden. Coming from Menon, highly respected as a man of few but well-chosen words, the comment set standards for the other estates in the company.

TOFFEE GAMBOLS ON THE LAWN WHILE NANDITA, HER MOTHER AND GRANDMOTHER LOOK ON. THIASHOLA BUNGALOW 1995

Vintage furniture filled the rooms of the estate's beautiful Victorian bungalow; its floors were laid with Italian tiles and its foyer windows were fitted with stained glass. It overlooked one of the richest ecosystems in the region, known as Silent Valley, the only place in the Western Ghats silent due to the absence of cicadas, a phenomenon as yet unexplained as is that of the Kuntipuzha river, which is said to remain perennially crystal clear. On a clear night, the plain below was beautifully decorated with tiny dots of light from the tribal settlements that lay spread across the region. The orchard adjoining the lawns was replete with peach, plum and pear trees that provided a haven for birds, bats, squirrels and langurs.

The best teas were made during wintery nights, and the aroma wafting out of the factory permeated the crisp dry air, a heady experience for visitors and residents of this tiny community. One night, as I set out for the factory to check on production, I observed movement in the orchard on the jail thottam. It appeared to be a mass of dry branches waving about, but I realised that it was the rugged, branching antlers of a massive Sambar stag. Looking closer I realised there were nearly a dozen of them, some appearing

From *Planting Directory of Southern India*, UPASI, Coonoor (1956)

yellow-brown and the others dark grey, with their shaggy coats shimmering in the brilliant moonlight. With short, dense, glistening manes and chestnut marks on their rumps, the majestic animals were contentedly foraging the fully-laden orchard. When I turned on the garden lights, they remained unperturbed. I opened the door and let Toffee out and in a while Gurang joined him too. As they raced around, yipping sharply, the deer who had at first tried to stand their ground, began to back off, turning around every now and then to evaluate the possibility of returning to their feast.

Later, on my way back from the factory, I saw the same herd now grazing in the dilapidated jail, picking the berries of lantana and wild raspberries in the compound, free to do as they wished, unlike the Chinese prisoners who had lived here decades ago. As the night progressed, they would wander down into the valley, to sip at the shores of Emerald or Avalanche lakes. By dawn they would be replaced by buffalos and bisons who would climb up the hills to graze in the nearby dales of the Upper Bhavani Grasslands.

ORIGINAL PHOTOGRAPH BY DR ARULNATHAN

SOMETHING ABOUT THE CHINESE PRISONERS

Excerpted from *Madras District Gazetteers, The Nilgiris,* Volume I by W Francis, Madras (1908) p184

In 1863 the opening of a plantation called Stanley at Melkundah, on the southern edge of the Kundahs, was also sanctioned. The cultivation of this, it may here be noted, was stopped in 1871, but the trees were left standing in order to ascertain whether they would flourish if left to themselves. They were speedily choked with jungle and the estate is now a ruin.

These estates were only very gradually planted up. In 1862, 31 acres were opened at Naduvattam; in 1863 planting on the Dodabetta and Wood properties was begun and Naduvattam was slightly extended; and apparently it was not until 1868 that the first planting was done on the Hooker estate. By that year cinchona seems to have been put down on a total of 355 acres in the four estates, but the official figures are conflicting and unreliable. Labour was so scarce that much of the work was done by convict labour; and the natives still call the Government plantations the 'Jail totes' and the old maps mark the sites of the temporary prisons in which the convicts were confined. Some of these men were Chinese who had been sent over to Madras jails from the Straits Settlements (where prison accommodation was scarce) and when their sentences expired a few of them settled down with Tamil wives at Naduvattam in a spot now known as 'the Chinese village' where they subsist as market-gardeners and dairymen.

NADUVATTAM

(Twenty-one miles from Ootacamund on Gudalur road)

Tiled building; hall and two bed-rooms, with bath rooms. Furnished with tables, chairs and cots, etc. A small amount of crockery, cutlery and cooking utensils. Kitchen, and stabling for four horses; also two coach godowns. Maly and sweeper attached. No supplies locally procurable. Re. 1 per day for a single person and Rs. 2 for a family, and As. 8 and Re. 1 for part of a day.

from *Bungalows and rest-houses in the Nilgiris, The Nilgiri Guide and Directory* by JSC Eagan Madras (1916) p163

CLIMBING THE ACACIA TREE

Edited excerpts from an article by MG Raghava Menon, one of the earliest Indian executives to join the tea industry in South India, in *Planter's Chronicle* September 1993. Adapted with kind permission from UPASI.

In 1939 and 1940, the beginning of the Second World War, many expatriates joined the war service, and this was when Indian nationals were increasingly appointed as executives in plantations owned by British companies. It was just these circumstances that created an opportunity for my entry into the plantation management. I was appointed as a 'Trainee Indian Assistant' to join duty on 1 February 1942. I recall vividly the interview I had with the late Mr JLH Williams outside the Thiashola Manager's Bungalow. He himself was, in addition to being the No 2 of the company, Tea Estates India (P) Ltd, in charge of Thiashola Estate whose permanent manager had left for war service. The interview was short, as prior to this, I had the privilege and opportunity of walking round the Carrington Division with him the previous week. My first posting was on Korakundah Estate, next door to Thiashola, and which in those days belonged to the company.

So, there I was on 1 February, attired in the typical planter's dress attending the morning muster at 7 am on a still winter day, shivering a little from the cold. On the previous day I had reported to the manager, a retired civilian expatriate and a war-time appointee himself. I was directed to see the field conductor, Mr Kesavan Nair, who would assist me in establishing myself in my house and guide me in the intricacies of plantation management. The house turned out to be a new labour quarters below the estate dispensary, comprising two rooms of area 12 feet by 10 feet and an outside kitchen (specially built for me) of half that size! I learnt later that the structure was meant to be used as a maternity ward. It was my temporary abode whilst a new assistant's bungalow was built, and which I did occupy two years later. Undaunted and displaying a forced cheer, I settled down with my meagre possessions of absolute necessities. The furnishing was spartan and there was no electricity, but the place was cosy with an old empty oil drum stove serving as a fireplace; firewood was plentiful. In fact (or so it seemed to me) there were more shade and fuel trees on that property than tea bushes! Below the house, there was a gentle and delightful stream on both sides of which bracken and broom grew wild. Many a Sunday, I have sat by its side and spent dreamy hours. There was no scope for extravagance on the allowance pay I was given, but it was sufficient to live in decent comfort and to keep a personal help.

For the first week, I was assigned the duty of supervising the loading and transporting of cattle manure from the pits to the fields – from 8am till 5pm with an interval of one hour for lunch. At the end of that week, I must have been reeking with the smell of dung, as I often lent a hand to lift the basket on the head or shoulder of the worker. On the whole, my work must have been considered satisfactory as I was shifted afterwards to supervise a different kind of work. And this was lopping or pollarding the acacia decurrens shade trees. This estate was mostly planted with this species as it was considered ideal to ward off the heavy frost.

Carrying a knife, which for a long time was part of my kit

on the daily rounds, I proceeded with the men to the work area. Watching the shaping of the trees to learn the trick of instructing properly, I saw the manager coming along with Mr Nair in trail. Preliminaries over, he said, "Now, young man, let me see how you cut those branches." I looked at him and he looked at me. My knees had already started behaving funnily. But how could I say that I had never climbed anything taller than my own height? Perhaps my job depended on this demonstration! So, saying a silent prayer, I climbed gingerly, sweat pouring out, and lo! I cut two branches, I know not with how many swipes. Mercifully, before any catastrophe took place, I was asked to come down. Nothing was said about my prowess then or after. Apparently he was satisfied.

Much later, I pondered over the purpose and meaning behind the way I was started on these jobs. One was that whatever kind of work is done, it has to be done well – "To do common things uncommonly well". Another was that there is no better way of disciplining oneself to know the nature of the work than doing it yourself. Climbing the tree also demonstrated to the workers that here was a future boss who did not hesitate to do the same work as they did; this indirectly helped gain a modicum of respect.

So started my career in planting. Amenities and comforts and social life were few, but there was little time to think about these for six days a week. Conditions were different in the estates situated in planting districts such as the Anamallais or High Ranges, but places like Korakundah and Kadamane were isolated indeed.

It may not be out of place at this stage to digress to some of the changes of the various aspects of plantations over the years. Unionism amongst the workers was unknown when I first joined. But, within a few years, the first of the

Workers' Union, affiliated to the INTUC was formed. To the credit of the union leaders, it must be said that they were a set of responsible people once the euphoria of power had worn off, until the time came when the unions splintered.

The training of young assistants depended largely on the field staff and management training and development, as is seen now, was non-existent. One's career advancement depended solely on one's efforts.

Looking at the profile of plantation companies, the change from a purely plantation-crop based company to a multi-product manufacturing unit is a major transition which has brought major changes in the pattern and quality of management and widened the scope of managerial opportunities with opportunities for intra-group and transnational movement of professionals.

MA BASITH KHAN, KM ACHIAH, S KRISHNAN, DR VENKATACHALAM, MG RAGHAVA MENON, N DHRAMARAJ (IN THE BACKGROUND) GP REDDY, S SURYANARAYANAN. DRESSED FOR AN EVENING OUT, IN THE JACKETS AND FLARED TIES OF THE TIME.
IMAGE COURTESY S SURYANARAYANAN, FORMER GENERAL MANAGER, TEI

OF JACKETS AND MANAGEMENT LESSONS

In the late sixties and early seventies, we were still following many British traditions, though tailcoats and dinner jackets were gradually giving way to lounge suits and the bandhgala. For Saturday nights at the club, however, gentlemen were expected to wear suits.

Shekar Daniel was a young manager of one of the tea estates at Highwavys. A brilliant man who played the game by the rules and was very popular socially, he never missed a club night. Prim and proper in his attire, he had worn an expensive suit that he had bought recently for the special Independence Day celebrations. The party progressed well past midnight and it was pretty late when Shekar got home. Next morning he was roused from deep sleep by the butler's knocks on his bedroom door; it was a working day and he was already late. Tea had been laid out on a table in the veranda and as Shekar approached it groggy eyed, his glance fell on an object laid flat on the lawn in front. Staring at it his curiosity turned to horror – could it possibly be the pelt of a dead animal? He walked up cautiously towards it and as he leaned forward to touch it, realised that it was his own expensive coat, laid out to dry in the hot sun. The bungalow servant, in an effort to impress the boss, had decided to give a thorough scrubbing to the suit with a cake of washing soap. With this, the linings had shrunk, the lapels had twisted and poor Shekar's expensive tweed coat was completely ruined. Instead of admonishing the servant for his foolish act, the gentlemanly Shekar appreciated his intention and counselled him that in future he would do better to take advise from the butler before indulging his proactive instincts.

AND THE PARTIES CONTINUE

The bonhomie among planters is everlasting! Bangalore is a hub, and many of us meet regularly at Ebony, the restaurant of Hotel Ivory Tower, owned by the Rajarams of Woodbriar. Here we update each other on the latest happenings in our previous companies and in the industry, relive funny stories from the past and renew our bonds. Off-site meetings provide a fun-filled getaway. In Coorg in November 2017, former Tea Estates India managers met along with their families at the Golf Club, Virajpet (seen below!) and we enjoyed the beauty and weather as well as the hospitality of our colleagues now living in Coorg. We now look forward to our meeting at the Ooty Club in October 2019, where this book will be launched.

A BOND TO HIS CUSTOMERS

The name Brooke Bond is said to have been coined by Arthur Brooke, owner of a tea shop, as his 'bond' to his customers to provide quality teas when he began wholesaling tea in UK in the 1870s. In 1903, Red Label was launched in colonial India. By 1957, Brooke Bond was probably the largest tea company in the world, with one third share of both the British and Indian tea markets.

Brooke Bond, agents of Tea Estates India, acquired the company and was later itself acquired by Unilever. During the twenty-two years that Unilever owned Tea Estates India (1984 to 2006), it made substantial investments, improving technology in the factories and fields, increasing both yields and quality of teas. Significant contribution was made in HRD, resulting in improved living and working conditions. Health-Safety-Environment (HSE) became a watchword of work ethics, and remarkable transformations were seen in the lifestyle of employees. Training and development across the board led to responsible and modern methods of management, and this resulted in excellent industrial relations.

ONE OF A SERIES OF ADVERTISEMENTS FOR TAJ MAHAL TEA C1979.
REPRODUCED WITH KIND PERMISSION FROM HINDUSTAN UNILEVER.

Time for a cuppa

We were cruising on the Thekkady Lake when the boat rocked and began to keel. The other couple in it with Rajam and me had stood up to get a closer look at the trunks of a group of elephants who were wading near the bank, and the boatman sternly instructed them to sit down, warning that the boat would capsize if they did not. Apologizing, they explained to us that they were visiting from Rajasthan and, where they lived, vegetation was sparse. Camels were common, but to see bathing elephants was a joy. We introduced ourselves and arranged to have dinner with the Bajorias at our hotel.

"My wife does not know how to make a good cup of chai," Ranjan confided as we chatted, "could you please tell her?" Rita was rolling her eyes with an indulgent look that said, "Well if this is the way he wants to enjoy his holiday, then let him."

I've lost count of the times people have asked me the best way to make tea. The thing is, taste is a subjective matter. When it comes to tea, the first thing you must do is choose the type of tea you like best, Orthodox or CTC. People who prefer flavour choose Orthodox teas that have more aroma and less strength. CTC teas, on the other hand, are noted for the strong cups they produce. Remember that the dust grades will give much stronger teas than the leafy Pekoes or Broken Pekoes.

Once you have selected your leaves, measure out a teaspoonful (5g); less if it is dust, and place it in a dry container, preferably a metal pot which will retain heat. Heat water in a kettle or pot and when it comes to a

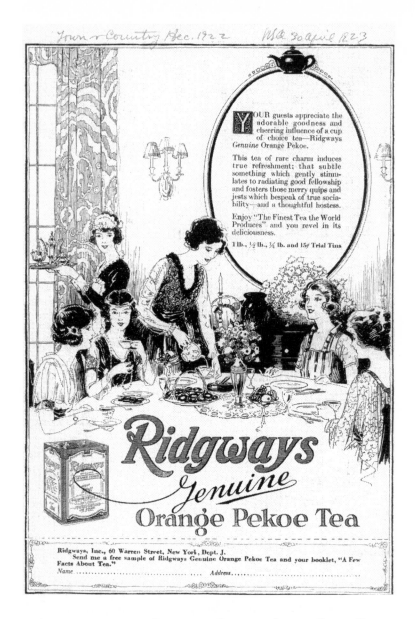

ADVERTISEMENT FOR RIDGWAYS GENUINE ORANGE PEKOE TEA,
RIDGWAYS INC., 60 WARREN STREET, NEW YORK, NEW YORK,
DECEMBER 1922 COURTESY OF HISTORIC NEW ENGLAND

boil, pour a cupful (150ml) over the dry tea leaves. Stir well and cover for five minutes to get a full infusion. Stir again before you decant the liquid into the serving cup, filtering it through a fine mesh sieve so that no leaves or dust fall into your cup. If you are particular about flavour, remember that the purer the water, the better the taste. Add milk and sugar if you wish, but do keep in mind that you will lose flavour if the milk is too hot. The best high-grown teas are generally drunk without milk and with a dash of lime or lemon instead, and unsweetened unless you insist on adding a dash of honey or pinch of sugar.

Ranjan was delighted with my recipe, and Rita was still wearing her patient look. When I asked how she makes tea, she told me that she boils fresh cow's milk in an aluminium vessel. Once the milk is nice and thick, she adds three teaspoons each of tea powder and sugar to make two cups, and after it boils, she continues to simmer it for a while. When she pours it out, she rushes a cup to Ranjan because he likes his tea piping hot.

I just could not resist explaining to them that cooking tea makes it astringent because the cell sap, the juice of the tea leaf, which has been locked in by the manufacturing process, dissolves in hot water but not in milk. As a result, tea boiled in milk is going to be astringent and will require a lot of milk and sugar to make it palatable. This will naturally change the taste completely.

After dinner, I made tea using my method for all of us. Ranjan drank with a lot of appreciation, but something told me that he was probably going to go home and tell his wife that he loved her tea best of all and that she did indeed know how to make the best chai ever.

THE NILGIRI HILLS

Excerpts from *Southern India* painted by Lady Lawley described by F.E. Penny, published by A.&C. Black London October (1914) p191-193

"The Madras Presidency is not made up entirely of scorching plains where dust-storms blow and devils ride the whirlwind in the hot season ; and where vegetation springs into leaf and bud under warm torrential downpour in the rainy season. It has its hills and plateau land easily accessible to the European who revels in subtropical climate rivalling the sunny slopes of Sicily.

"The Nilgiri Hills form part of the Western Ghats and lie south of the Mysore plateau. For years they were seen from a distance by the Englishmen, a line of mysterious ethereal blue like a serrated wall of forest. Those who approached found them pathless and repellant, too vast, too impenetrable to invite the explorer, who was bound to the plains by his duty to his employer, the old John Company.

"It was not until the year 1800 that they were invaded by a European. Dr. Francis Buchanan, following the tracks used by the native hill people, climbed up from the Bowani valley. He was not in search of a climate, nor had he any thought of a sanatorium for his fellow-men. His object was mineral and vegetable products that might be turned to account in the enormous market that the Company had created during the last two hundred years. Gold, silver, iron, diamonds, timber, gall-nuts, ebony, sandalwood ; anything, in short, that could be dealt with commercially.

"What he found was of inestimable value, although it could not be sent home to be sold with the spices of the East. It was the soma, the nectar of the Indian gods, the life-restoring breezes of the hill-tops that have often robbed death of its prey during the last hundred years."

Following this discovery, in 1818 "Kindersley and Whish, of the Company's civil service" climbed the same difficult track, encouraged to persevere only on the strength of Buchanan's report:

"They passed through the dry thorny zone of scrubby deciduous jungle, which falls an easy prey to the forest fire. Gradually, as they mounted, the bamboos grew less dense ; the cactus and then the palm disappeared, and they entered the fairy land of fern, perennial evergreen, and the giant forest tree. They came upon bud and blossom. The cool air blew down from crag and moorland above with the revivifying effect of champagne. They emerged on the downs above the spot where Ootacamund now stands, and with their advent the Englishman had at last 'come to stay.'

"At that time it was the custom for those in the Company's service whose health had failed to take a trip to the Cape for change of air. The two men recognized the fact that here, close at hand, was a better sanatorium than the coast of South Africa could offer. Here was a spot that might be reached, if roads were opened, in as many hours as it took days to get to Cape Town. Here the delicate drooping children and fading wives might be brought to recuperate their strength with little trouble and small expense."

THEY LAID THE BASE FOR US

Planters Old: an **excerpt from** *A Planting Century, The first hundred years of the United Planters' Association of Southern India 1893-1993* **by S Muthiah, Affiliated East West Press (1993) p379-380**

There have been three ages of planters in the hills of Southern India. The first was the age of the pioneers that might be said to be anywhere from the 1820s to the beginning of the 20th century. Those were the days of the great individualists, men who may be described as Characters, to whom more than half the joy was opening up new land. It was the age of the proprietary planter who, as the century ended, gave way to companies and accepted employment in them or, like FG Richardson, who took up residence in a shack along a godforsaken road, went mad and died. It was also the age of coffee's rise and fall, making paupers of many of them, and of a desperate search for another crop which would mend their fortunes. They could not have been good years, nor could the niceties of life have been expected of such rough and ready men, always under pressure and ever faced with uncertainty. It was a period when there were several doubts expressed not only over planting but over planters themselves. The picture of an avaricious East India Company encouraging the planters to pluck as must as possible from the rich soil of India was far from true, at least in South India, where the dream of Empire began in the minds of men who came to these shores as coastal traders. That the planters - most of them hardy Scots - did eventually wrest a living from the land was often despite the authorities.

The second age began with the example James Finlay set in the second half of the 1890s and which was followed by several other companies, though, in many years, especially in the coffee districts of Mysore and

Coorg the rugged believer in self-reliance continued to be an enthusiastic entrepreneur. With the company estates came the Managers, Superintendents and Assistants - not to mention the lowly 'creeper' - all working for the company in an environment where they still had to open out land while simultaneously cultivating - or, in most cases, rehabilitating - what was on it. This was the age when most of these planters had to learn about tea, discover for themselves how to manage a large labour force in alien surroundings and bring about a degree of comfortable living not only for themselves but for their workers too. It was an era of hard, unremitting labour with few to help and fewer facilities on land.

It is these two ages that are the years of Planters Old. The age of Planters New did begin in the late Thirties and early Forties, but World War II created an unreal situation and it was only after 1948 and Independence that the Planter New came into his own. It was an age where gradually estates were passing from British ownership to Indian ownership, then from field management by expatriates to field management by Indians who had as much acquaintance with plantations as the pioneers. It was also an age where what had seemed glorified farming and part of the agricultural sector was seen as an industry that could be expanded substantially to make it a major contributor to the Exchequer. As this thought grew in the 1980s and 1990s, there has come the need to look at Planters Tomorrow.

"THE CHINESE SAY IT'S BETTER TO BE DEPRIVED OF FOOD FOR THREE
DAYS THAN TEA FOR ONE."
KHALED HOSSEINI, *A Thousand Splendid Suns*

The haunted bungalow

Memories from Carolyn Hollis

It is over fifty years since I arrived at High Forest Estate in the Anamallai Hills, having married the Manager, David Hollis, in England just three days before.

It was the last, most remote estate in the district; communications were sparse at that time; I had been warned it might be lonely and I wouldn't be able to speak to any of my family for the next two years.

India was so far away – not just in distance but in a whole way of life and I was elated to be getting to know and to become a part of it.

My new home was a vast bungalow with high ceilings and long passages. As it was the first month of a vigorous monsoon, it was some time before the clouds and mist cleared and I could appreciate the garden and magnificent mountain setting. The damp and the dreaded leeches had gone, the sun shone and, everything was fine – except …

There was something strange about the front of the house. David told me he had come back one night and had the strange feeling that the bungalow was being pressed down by a weight. In the front room, his two dogs were sitting close together, shivering and staring up at the ceiling. I soon realised there was something odd about the hall area. We genuinely thought sometimes that someone had come to the front door, and we had seen the door handle move.

One evening our servant John came to the door, as usual, we assumed, with the tappal – our mail delivery. But he didn't come in. We just got a glimpse, a wisp of his dhoti as he turned. But he wasn't there. The long passage was empty.

There was a huge wooden clothes hanger in the hall, but I

noticed that when you hung something up carefully in the evening, it would be on the floor the next morning.

I woke one evening feeling a little strange and hearing someone breathing. It was eerie. It happened again – I was told that someone was probably sleeping at the back and the vast space above the ceiling was magnifying the sound of breathing.

Then someone walked along the veranda outside our bedroom in the middle of the night. I found it oddly frightening. This was when I knew something was happening to me alone. There was no point in waking my husband for reassurance. That was the hard part. The next day I looked at the veranda. Beneath it was a monsoon drain – pipes led across it fixed with metal bars. No one could walk along there with regular footsteps. But the previous night someone had.

My worst night; David was away. Our son Peter was a baby in a basket crib on a stand between my bed and the window. I woke to a sense of that fear that came more strongly than before, like some warning from outside the window. I had to get my son and grab him away from something I didn't understand. The worst part was that as desperately as I needed to go to him, I couldn't move. I was transfixed. When the fear diminished. I grabbed him from his cot and ran down the passage to a room at the back of the house where everything was calm and safe.

When Peter was a toddler, we asked him one day who he was talking to. "That lady over there," he said. Another time when asked what people he liked he pointed to a large mirror in a dark corner and said "Those people there".

Of course I knew that children conjure up strange stories and have imaginary friends. But when these happen in a place like High Forest – well, you begin to wonder...

I told local people about my experiences but they didn't seem to understand or try and reassure me. I tried to convince myself that there was nothing untoward except in my story teller's ingenuity. It worked for a while, until – a visitor who had lived in the district called and asked, "Does that man still walk up and down outside your bedroom window at night?"

Then I met someone who had once lived in the house "Was there something odd about the hall – did you find things fell off the hat stand in the night?" That didn't happen any more. Once I had had it moved into another room, things stayed neatly where they were put.

Some one later asked me if I found the house unsettling. Why? "The last planter's wife had days when she just could not stay in the bungalow. I don't know why. We were told not to tell you..."

A few years later, from Seaforth, I took my children to stay with friends in the Anamallais. The baby stayed with the friends and I took my three-year-old Peter to lunch with Bob and Situ Savur in the High Forest bungalow.

Peter, a gregarious child was very excited when I told him there were children there for him to play with. And toys? Yes, and toys!

I parked at the front of the house, we got out and were welcomed. He was silent. He faltered near the porch. He would not enter. He was tempted, cajoled, to no avail. Eventually the kindly but curious servants brought him his lunch outside. He solemnly sat alone and ate it there.

He could not go into the house. He still doesn't know why.

And nor do I.

Born in a post office

Memories from Saaz Aggarwal

I have no idea whether the High Forest manager's bungalow is haunted, but I do know that it is a very special and in fact historic place for my family because my brother Ravi was born there in July 1963, not too long after the Hollis family moved to Seaforth.

When my mother was expecting me, she went to stay with her parents in Bombay, and I was delivered in due course by Dr BN Purandare at his nursing home so close to Chowpatty beach that to set sail and embark on a long voyage straight away, all we would have had to do was cross the road. But to have Ravi, she somehow managed to convince my dad that she had no intention of even leaving the house.

When it was time for the baby, my dad called Dr Menon, the estate doctor, to be on standby while he drove out to fetch Dr Manchi Disawalla who was stationed at the nearby

THE HIGH FOREST MANAGER'S BUNGALOW.
ORIGINAL PHOTOGRAPH BY CAROLYN HOLLIS

town of Mudis. Dr Disawalla was the best doctor in the district and he and his wife Gool, who was also an excellent doctor, were very good friends of my parents. Anandan, our butler, was instructed to arrange for large pots of boiling water to sterilize the instruments, and for hot wet towels and cold wet towels. Almost before all this was ready, the baby arrived.

High Forest is a rainy place – second only to Cherrapunji, as my mother used to say back then. In the monsoon, clothes wouldn't dry, biscuits got soggy in seconds, shoes would be lined with fungus within hours of taking them off. My dad would come back from the fields with leeches clinging to his long socks. It had been raining non-stop but the morning the baby was born, after weeks shrouded by clouds, the sun came out personally to welcome him. Besides, it was a Sunday. So they named him Ravi.

Two weeks later, my mum was back at the club to play an evening game of bridge, and her partner was Gool Shavaksha (the daughter of Sir Dinshah Mulla, whose statue

SITU, RAVI AND SAAZ OUTSIDE THEIR HOME WITH ANOTHER CHILD, HIGH FOREST, 1966. ON THE RIGHT, THE SAME HOUSE IN 2014.

stands outside the Bombay High Court). Mrs Shavaksha, who was visiting from Bombay to be with her daughter Zarine Kothavala, complimented my mother saying, "You've lost a lot of weight since I last saw you!"

"Yes," she responded with satisfaction, "I've just had a baby."

In 1968, my father was transferred from High Forest to Prospect. Ravi was not yet five. But High Forest would always stay with him. On his passport, 'place of birth' would always be 'High Forest, Mudis Post Office'; in a country filled with so many thousands of remote places, and so many millions of letter-writers and money-order-senders, a post office was your infallible indicator of location.

Years later, well into middle age, I told this story to a former schoolmate, Venky Muthiah of the luxurious Sinna Dorai Bungalow Resorts, and he located Simon in Valparai. Simon, who had worked with my father in High Forest, went back there to take photos of the Manager's bungalow for me – and here they are. The world had changed and so had Ravi's first home: once elegant and beautifully maintained, it was now in a state of decay, a suitable place for a haunting, with any ghosts that may have lingered now left to their own devices.

Saaz and Ravi outside their home in 1967. On the right, the same house in 2014. From Saaz's album.

Dog eating panther

More memories from Saaz Aggarwal

We left Prospect in 1973, and I have been back to visit twice over the decades. The road is so broken down that it is almost inaccessible. West Downs is unoccupied and in shambles, and the fields of tea are heart-wrenchingly overgrown and unkempt. The table tennis table is gone from our playroom but the blackboard our dad had painted across one wall for us is still there. So is the carved rosewood wardrobe in my bedroom, and, astonishingly, the sitting room curtains have remained unchanged. Is there anyone left any more to mourn, on bitterly cold winter mornings,

BOB AND SITU SAVUR IN THE WEST DOWNS SITTING ROOM C1971. THIS PHOTO MAY HAVE BEEN A PRESENT FROM THE JAPANESE ENGINEERS (WHO APPEAR ON PAGE 87) AS THE ORIGINAL LOOKS LIKE A POLAROID. ON THE RIGHT ARE VEDA, AJAY, EKTA AND AMAN AGGARWAL (SAAZ'S FAMILY) SAME ROOM, SAME CURTAINS, 1998.

the acres of tea burnt black by frost as they always were, a few times each year, year after year? Or are the winters less cold than they used to be? On both visits, I met people who remembered my dad – the dorai who would ride through the fields with our dog, Chittu, balancing regally on pillion. As my father started the bike and rolled it out, he'd pause and look around him, and that would be Chittu's signal to run and leap up.

My brother Ravi and I commuted from Prospect to St Hilda's School in Ooty for two years, trapped in the backseat of our red Standard Herald for an hour each way (Chinappan had been instructed to drive carefully), with no recourse but to quarrel and pull each other's hair when it got too stressful. Long stretches of eucalyptus saplings had been recently planted along the way, and we enlivened the monotony by competing to spot and count the number of boards that said 'E Globulus' on them. Chamraj Sagar had a little island on it and that, of course, was where Robinson Crusoe lived, but somehow we never caught sight of him. Driving past vast rolling downs, we decided to build a large colony on them and invite all our Bombay friends and relatives – whom we only got to see once a year – to live there so that we'd have more company than just each other's. There was a sheep farm coming up at Sandynalla. One Sunday we went to visit the Sethna family – Nosh and Freny, Aban and Homi – at Dunsandle (which, as page 141 of this book tells us, is one of the very first estates to have been planted in the Nilgiris), and Ravi fell in the pond.

I began working on a book based on plantation life in April 2013, first interviewing Uncle Sin (NSV Sinniah), who had started his career as a tea planter in Ceylon before moving to E&A, followed by a few more with other Ooty locals that year. In March 2015, I interviewed Ravindran and Ram Adige in Bangalore, both former E&A employees and colleagues of my father. It was a wonderful session, but the book took a back seat to other projects. So, when Ravindran told me in June 2019 that he had a collection of stories he wanted my help in publishing, I agreed at once and have enjoyed the process of weaving in context and fleshing them out with memories from him and others, including my own. Working on this book took me back to an idyllic childhood, its pristine air-quality, vistas of sloping valleys of smooth green from the sitting-room windows, brilliant night skies, and a certain formal grandeur and privileged way of living compounding the fundamental isolation of plantation life. The sunsets at Prospect were spectacular: one time, driving towards the fork in the road that led into the estate, the sky ahead was streaked with clouds that carried every colour of the rainbow, the entire spectrum from purple to red, a sight that remains fresh in my mind nearly fifty years later.

SEATED: DHARMAM (HIS SON BIMAL RAJASEKHAR IS STANDING NEXT TO HIM), SAAZ, SITU, BOB AND RAVI SAVUR. FROM SAAZ'S ALBUM. HIGH FOREST, 1967

Out of the blue I remembered Dharmam, a mechanic at Prospect. I phoned Victor to ask and he said, "Of course I remember him, he was your dad's favourite!" Victor went on to give me a few examples of Dharmam's ingenuity:

> At Prospect we used motorized power sprayers and to start them, we had to tie a rope around the motor and pull. But it was so cold right around the year that a simple pull never worked. We had to keep pulling, it took a lot of time, a lot of tries and a lot of strength, and they still wouldn't start. Until Dharmam came up with a brilliant idea: he hooked the rope to a V-belt on one of the machines. When the machine was turned on, its rapid revolution started the sprayer in no time.

As I wrote this down, an image emerged from the deep recesses of my memory: the door to 'Aladdin's Cave', a dark and perhaps windowless restricted-entry room in the Prospect factory, Dharmam's secret stockroom. When anything needed fixing, Dharmam would retreat into the cave and emerge carrying a piece of scrap or spare or strange-looking tool, and get it working in a jiffy. Victor remembered that he never threw anything away; that he used discarded lorry shock absorbers to make stools to sit on. My brother and I even had a car, which Dharmam had made using discarded metal sheets, a marvel of technology with a working steering wheel, a discarded lorry horn and discarded bicycle pedals.

FROM *PLANTING DIRECTORY OF SOUTHERN INDIA*, UPASI, COONOOR (1956)

257

Dharmam was a genius and, in different circumstances, could have been an inventor who formed the backbone of a national space mission or corporate R&D department.

His father, PA Charles, had gone to work at Dunsinane Estate, Ceylon, and rose to be teamaker there. After some years he quit to return to the family home in Nagercoil, Tamilnadu, and subsequently worked as teamaker at High Forest and Seaforth. Dharmam, well qualfied and highly skilled, joined High Forest in 1954. These facts I learnt from his son Rajappa. I had made many attempts to locate Dharmam's children, and it seemed like a miracle to do so just days before this book went to print – particularly because, on that 2016 visit to Prospect, I had been informed (mistakenly, as it turned out) that Dharmam was no more.

DHARMAM'S CHILDREN, RAJAPPA CHARLES AND BIMAL RAJASEKHAR, IN CARS FABRICATED BY THEIR FATHER. RAJAPPA GREW UP TO BE AN ENGINEER, AND BIMAL IS A DOCTOR WITH A MASTER'S DEGREE IN PUBLIC HEALTH FROM LONDON SCHOOL OF ECONOMICS. THEIR MOTHER HELEN, SEEN IN THE PHOTO ON THE LEFT, WAS A MUCH BELOVED TEACHER IN THE ESTATE SCHOOLS. DHARMAM RETIRED FROM SEAFORTH IN 1987 AND THEY CONTINUED LIVING THERE UNTIL SHE RETIRED FOUR YEARS LATER.

In fact, Dharmam celebrated his ninetieth birthday in April 2019. And in September I learnt from him that it was a rotorvane that took Peter Sausman's finger. A rotorvane is the machine in which tea leaves are loaded after going through the rollers, forced through a barrel by a screw-type rotating shaft with vanes at its centre. Peter evidently got too close. He lost a finger, but his sense of humour, as Ravindran describes earlier in the book, stayed on.

Visiting Prospect in 2016 I had asked after Hutcha too, and was told that he too was no more. Hutcha was a lorry driver in our time, and of English blood, as I deduced from an email from Denis Mayne in 2015, followed by a conversation with others who knew. Denis now lives in Belfast, and I had come across his post 'When I was in India' on a Bangor Aye blog, in which he described his initiation on Prospect, less gentle than Ravindran's would be a decade later, with a manager who sent him off saying:

> I'll see you on Friday. In the mean time you are in charge of four hundred acres of tea and four hundred men. Only one man speaks English and you can't believe a word he says. Good Luck!

I was delighted to get connected to him through the blog, and through him to Carolyn Hollis; their words and photos have brought parts of this book alive. As for Hutcha's biological father, you could probably spot him in the photo on the last page, one of the last grand collections of British and Indian tea planters c1958. Most of them are no more.

Chittu is long gone too. One evening at Kodanad in the 1980s, he went off as usual to run around and do dog things, and never came back. "Dog eating panther," as the butler English of our days described it, not an unusual end for an estate dog, much mourned by all of us, especially my dad, who would now have to ride out to the fields on his own.

How it all began

By the nineteenth century, the British had become a nation of tea drinkers. The cultivation of tea was still a monopoly of China and tea chests arriving from China were sold through auctions attended by tea brokers, their clients and London merchants, over which the East India Company exerted a monopoly. As demand rose, costs rose too. The Company began to subsidise the resulting drain on their profits by introducing an equally addictive substance into China, opium, which they cultivated in India and exported. This made tycoons of many – including, it is said, James Matheson (whose name may ring a bell to readers of this book). The Chinese government responded with indignation and two 'opium wars' took place.

The desperate urge for tea led to another interesting story. Though making tea is easy, its manufacture is a complex process with various precise stages, which depend to an extent on atmospheric conditions too. This remained a Chinese secret until, in the mid-1800s, the adventurer Robert Fortune, "a plant hunter, a gardener, a thief, a spy," as Sarah Rose described him in her 2010 book For All the Tea in China – came along and figured it out.

By this time, the British had noticed that tea was indigenous to Assam and had begun cultivating it there. They then set up plantations in Ceylon and subsequently in South India too. According to the website of the Assam government's Krishna Kanta Handiqui State Open University, the first consignment of Assam tea was put up at the London

Auction on 10 January, 1839, the first auction sale of Indian tea in the international market. The British were not just drinking tea, they were also doing a brisk trade in it. Scott C Levi writes, in The Indian Diaspora in Central Asia and its Trade, (Brill 2002 p51):

> "in the 1840s, Mohan Lal noted that ... tea was commonly transported from India to Bukhara via the overland routes traversing Khulum. Later that century, in 1869, another Russian author reported that tea was commonly transported from Bombay up the Indus river to Peshawar, and from there to Kabul, Balkh, Qarshi and Bukhara to Tashkent. An English traveller subsequently reported that, because of a breakdown in trade relations with China, roughly 10,000 camel loads of tea or nearly five million pounds, was annually transported from India to Bukhara. By 1880, this had dropped considerably, although, according to the figures presented by Rasul-Zade, Bukhara still imported more than three million pounds of tea annually."

To grow the new industry, the British media published encouraging articles and books, painting an attractive picture and giving detailed descriptions of life in the plantations. The Neilgherry Tea Planter by James McPherson (Higginbotham Madras 1870), for instance, is a do-it-yourself manual of how to grow tea. It encourages planters to buy waste land and start planting. Information about what is required, how to build, heating using wood boilers, the process of black tea manufacture, the difference between green tea and black tea, the yield that can be expected, the annual calendar in terms of climate-related activities, prices and many more topics are explained in detail. These campaigns led to young British men 'coming out' to try their luck and pioneer something new. Plunging themselves into a different world, they gave all they had, and many succeeded. Many estate names in South India are derived from Tamil words. Many also reflect the nostalgia of the pioneering English and Scottish planters: Arran View, Brooklands, Craigmore, Glenburnie and many more; the 1966 Tea Board India tea directory lists more than sixteen estates with 'glen' in their names.

The first commercial planting commenced in 1875 in Peermade. In 1878, James Finlay began to develop the Kannan Devan Hills in Munnar, in 1889 planting started in Wynaad and in 1897 in the Anamallais.

Tea seeds of either the broad-leaved Assam variety or the narrow-leaved China variety were planted in mud pots in tea nurseries to produce seedlings which were transplanted to the field when good root and shoot development were

BULKING TEA IN THE WAREHOUSES OF THE EAST & WEST INDIA DOCK COMPANY, LONDON, 1874. BULKING WAS A PROCESS NECESSARY ESPECIALLY WITH INDIAN TEA, AS ON THE JOURNEY THE SMALLER LEAVES AND DUST WORKED THEIR WAY TO THE BOTTOM OF THE CHESTS.
OXFORD SCIENCE ARCHIVE/PRINT COLLECTOR/GETTY IMAGES

established. The plants that grew from seedlings were robust, but once flowers were cross-pollinated to produce seeds, quality could not be ensured. It was only when clones came into use that clonal teas, propagated in nurseries through two-inch shoots with a healthy leaf from a model plant, produced reliable quality with flavour, yield, and resistance to disease. This only happened in South India in the 1960s and in the decades ahead, plantations continued to evolve.

In the meanwhile, as tea production increased, enthusiastic sales efforts were made too. Newspaper advertisements appeared in the USA in the 1890s, and one of them, entitled *A Third Little Story for the Tea Table,* reads:

> A menace to health are the adulterated, nerve-disturbing teas of China and Japan. Teas of India and Ceylon are strictly pure. Made of young leaves which contain the essence of the whole plant. When using India or Ceylon Tea, care should be taken to put in the pot **only about half** of what is used in the case of China or Japan teas. This is because of its greater strength, giving really "two cups in one." **Use fresh boiled and boiling water – do not allow the tea to draw more than three to five minutes, according to taste**, and you will have perfect tea. **Never boil tea**. There is no trouble or perplexity in life which cannot be alleviated by a cup of this soothing, upholding and invigorating beverage. It is less stimulating and more refreshing than coffee. It and sleep are "nature's sweet restorers." You may not like the first cup because of its novelty (that is, its purity); the second you will find tolerable, the third you will like, and then you want it, and there is no relapse.

Some of the tea plantations were owned by individuals, but joint-stock sterling companies were registered in the United Kingdom from the 1830s. Records show how proprietors gradually gave way to corporates. In 1916, a company called Seaforth Plantations owned Beddington, Ossington, Pykara Falls, Belle Vue and Riverside; by 1956, these had all become divisions of Liddellsdale and Prospect, which

THE SOUTH TRAVANCORE TEA COMPANY, LIMITED.

Formed July, 1896.

CAPITAL.—*Authorised*—£50,000 in 5,000 shares of £10 each, divided into 2,500 6% Preference and 2,500 Ordinary shares.

Issued—£27,500 in 1,375 shares of each denomination.

Preference shares are cumulative, and have priority as to Capital as well as dividend.

Directors.

T. C. OWEN, Esq.

A. V. HOLLAND, Esq.   NEILL GRAEME CAMPBELL, Esq.

H. M. KNIGHT, Esq.

Bankers.

NATIONAL BANK OF INDIA, LIMITED.

Agents in London.

Messrs. ROWE, WHITE & Co.

Secretary.   *Offices.*

E. LANGLEY, Esq.   16, PHILPOT LANE, LONDON, E.C.

HISTORY.—The Prospectus was dated 27th July, 1896, and stated that the Company was formed for the purpose of taking over, as going concerns, as from the 1st July of that year, the Venture, Arnichardi and Neddumpara Estates, and also from 1st September the Nagamally Estate, all situated in South Travancore, Southern India, and comprising a total area of about 2,304 acres, of which about 850 were under tea, 125 under coffee, and 6 under nutmegs. They stand at an average elevation of 1,100 ft. Nearly all the tea is in full bearing. The Nagamally, Arnichardi and Neddumpara Estates are freehold ; Venture is held under lease at a nominal quit-rent from the Government, and is renewable at the option of the Company. No Debentures will be issued against the properties except with the assent of a majority of two-thirds of the Preference shareholders. The purchase price of the Venture, Arnichardi and Neddumpara Estates was fixed at £26,000, payable as to £10,000 in Ordinary shares and £3,250 in Preference shares, and the balance, £12,750, in cash ; the Company paid costs and charges incidental to its formation. The Nagamally Estate was subsequently bought for £4,000.

ACCOUNTS.—None yet issued.

DIRECTORS' QUALIFICATION.—£100.

TRANSFER FORM.—Ordinary ; Fee, 2s. 6d. per deed.

Prior to this, the Southern India Tea Estates Company Limited was incorporated in March 1895, apparently the first in South India, with an authorised capital of £40,000. Its directors were William Forbes Laurie, Esq., Theo Charles Owen, Esq., and Alfred Valentine Holland Esq., and its offices were also in 16, Philpot Lane, London EC. The company was incorporated with the purpose of acquiring, working, and developing the Kaduwa Karnum Tea Estates. It also acquired, as from 1 January 1896, the Glen Mary and Westerton Estates, all in the district of Peermade, Travancore, and at elevations of between 3,300 and 4,200 feet above sea level. Excerpted from *Tea Producing Companies of India and Ceylon* Gow Wilson and Stanton, London (1897) p91-93.

were owned by E&A. In 1916, Prospect was owned by WR Arbuthnot, Sir John's grandfather, and the privately-held Woodbrook had been absorbed into it too. The collapse of Arbuthnot Bank in Madras in 1906 brought any number of planters in South India to ruin, but the investigations of how this affected the distribution of ownership is outside the scope of this book. The corporates, with boards that sat in the UK, employed local agents to implement the policies and vision of the companies' boards.

A slump during the First World War (1914-1918) was quickly overcome, and the industry made rapid progress with the export market expanding and with the increase in consumption of tea in India. This led, in 1919-1920, to a business-cycle low resulting from excessive supply. Some sterling companies divested, enabling wealthy Indians to acquire plantations. The world economic depression of the early 1930s also affected the tea industry.

Tea production reduced during the Second World War (1939-1945), when estate managers left to serve in the armed forces and labour in Assam and West Bengal were diverted to the construction of roads and bridges. Post-war inflation made it necessary to review the treatment of golden-goose labour, and to improve conditions and increase wages. The trend continued with Indian-influenced government planning which recommended that profit be harnessed to social needs.

As post-war production costs continued to rise and repatriation of profits reduced, some of the early proprietary owners sold to Indians. And, as Independence approached, the fear of nationalisation caused more such divestments.

With Independence came the stark awareness of a depleted economy and dire shortage of foreign exchange.

This necessitated government control of foreign exchange operations and the restriction of imports of any commodity required for tea processing and manufacturing. Before the Second World War, a large percentage of tea was marketed in London. The London Auction Centre reopened only in 1951, so auctions were held in Calcutta in 1946 and Colombo in 1947 to dispose of the surplus. As tea production continued to grow globally and new markets emerged, auction centres were established in Cochin, Amritsar, Coonoor, Guwahati, Siliguri, Jalpaiguri, Coimbatore, Mombasa, Chittagong, Limbe and Djakarta. Over time, these led to a dilution of the volumes sent to London and in 1998, the historic London Tea Auction was closed. Today, India's six auction centres conduct auctions electronically.

The tea industry has traditionally been labour intensive. Mechanisation was introduced in the fields with hand-held plucking shears in the late 1980s and 1990s. This reduced labour costs – but the impact of yield per hectare was insignificant and the indiscriminate shearing reduced the premium flavour.

ADAPTED FROM *TARESH THE TEA PLANTER* BY PAPAS, LONDON 1968

Until the 1930s, tea was a drink enjoyed largely in Britain and made from high-grown leaves using the 'orthodox' form of manufacture. When another manufacturing method called Crush-Tear-Curl or CTC made an appearance, it spread rapidly from Assam to South India and its popularity spread across the world. The tea produced by CTC made twice as many strong cups as orthodox did; it also soon became the tea of choice to the masses.

With changing times, the drink once so much in demand that it led to wars and espionage reduced in popularity. As the awareness of the limitations of modern medicine grew, natural remedies became popular. When tea became labelled a caffeine drink, it became less attractive to new-age thinkers and was replaced in many homes by herbal infusions. However, the truth is that tea is in fact a miracle drink replete with anti-oxidants, and the industry must take another firm stand to restore this perception!

TEA: INDIA'S NATIONAL DRINK!
SAAZ AGGARWAL, PUNE, SEPTEMBER 2019

M RAVINDRAN'S ACKNOWLEDGEMENTS

This book owes a lot to my wife, who has been part and parcel of my experiences during our long stint in the verdant tea plantations of the western ghats. At various stages of writing, she has been a critic – a virtual voice of the unseen reader. For these I thank her.

Our son, Arjun, gave me a voice recorder one day last year, to speak anecdotes and episodes into. Although this didn't happen, the book did take shape. Thanks Arjun for providing the impetus.

Nandita, our daughter, has been after me to write ever since I hung up my boots nearly two decades ago. What was supposed to be blog posts eventually became a compendium of tea tales. I thank her for her conviction in my writing skills.

Another person who fuelled the fire right from the very first article and consistently through the process has been my brother Unni, to whom I owe a great deal for all that he has done for the book. Thank you for the encouragement and unstinted support.

Saaz has brought so much to the table that I am deeply indebted. A book of this nature owes a lot to the wealth of material and visual imagery that have been painstakingly woven into the story. To Saaz, Ravi, and Veda – my former boss Bob Savur's daughter, son and granddaughter – a big thank you for your whole-hearted and meticulous contribution.

I have received overwhelming motivation from former colleagues, planter friends, and a host of associates for which my appreciation goes on record.

I acknowledge with gratitude the time the reviewers spared to vet drafts of this book, providing criticism and valuable inputs.

ABOUT M RAVINDRAN

Ravindran was born in Elapully Village, Palakkad District, Kerala in July 1947. When he was ten, his family moved to Madras and he completed his schooling at Madras Christian College High School. Graduating from Loyola College, Madras, he joined a British-owned plantation company near Ooty and there began the saga recounted in this book.

His career in the Nilgiris, Anamallais and Meghamalai lasted till the turn of the century. Besides planting and maintaining tea, he was also in charge of factories, managing and manufacturing high-quality teas. After thirty-five years of very satisfying service, he hung up his boots in 2001. The next two decades in Bangalore saw him in roles as varied as training and development for the construction sector, general manager for the Biotech Apex body, and volunteering for a speech and hearing organization. He began writing in response to requests from friends and young relatives to share his experience as a tea planter. His inherent love for nature and the flora and fauna of the region is evident all through his stories.

RAVINDRAN LIVES WITH HIS WIFE RAJAM IN BANGALORE. THEY ARE SEEN AT THE CENTRE OF THIS PHOTOGRAPH WITH THEIR DAUGHTER'S FAMILY, WHO LIVE IN KANNUR, ON THE LEFT: VIJAY NAIR, MADHAV AND NANDITA; AND THEIR SON'S FAMILY, WHO LIVE IN FLORIDA, USA, ON THE RIGHT: MEGHNA MOHAN, NEEL AND ARJUN.

PROSPECT ESTATE, C1958. FROM SAAZ'S ALBUM.